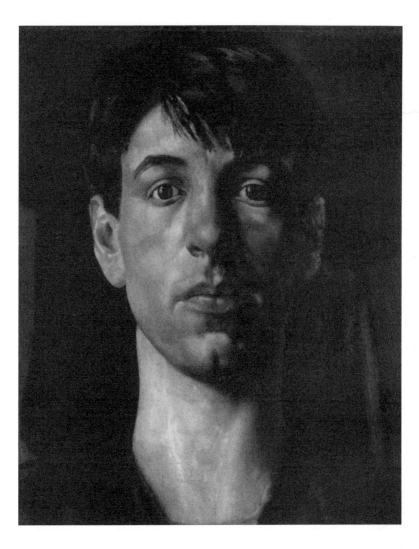

Living Here

David Helwig

We acknowledge the support of the Canada Council for the Arts, the Ontario Arts Council and the Government of Canada through the Book Publishing Industry Development Program for our publishing activities.

Parts of this book have appeared, often in different form, on CBC Radio and in *Arts Atlantic, Canadian Forum, Canadian Geographic, Canadian Notes and Queries, The Gazette, The Globe and Mail* and *The Imperial Oil Review*.

ISBN 0 7780 1165 8 (hardcover)
ISBN 0 7780 1166 6 (softcover)

Cover art by Sir Stanley Spencer courtesy Tate Gallery
Book design by Michael Macklem

Printed in Canada

PUBLISHED IN CANADA BY OBERON PRESS

ONTARIO ARTS COUNCIL
CONSEIL DES ARTS DE L'ONTARIO

Contents

Robert and Edward

Carry your grief alone,
No other wants it,
Each man has his own,
A fool flaunts it
—Robert Finch.

The bar will close.
The men will go
each one along
his path of snow
—Edward Lacey.

They died in the same month, June 1995, in Toronto, where I had known them both nearly 40 years before, and where they had known each other.

Fall of 1994, a street near Allen Gardens, large brick houses, old trees. Toronto. In this neighbourhood, still, Toronto as you see it in the brilliant moody paintings of Albert Franck. I went in a door at street level, and one or two men were standing around in a common area with a coffee-maker and some old chairs, and then I went up a dark staircase, two floors, and there was a long narrow hall with a window at the end, and along the hall, closed doors. I made my way to the third or fourth door on the right and knocked and waited.

It was a boarding-house for burnt-out cases, drink, drugs, madness, failure, and behind the closed door, Edward Lacey was asleep. Two days before, I'd come here for the first time to find him. I was editing a collection of his letters to Henry Beissel, and while he'd signed a letter of agreement with Henry about the existence of the book, I now had a contract ready, and I knew that if someone didn't actually deliver it into his hands, it would vanish into the disorder of his life. That day I'd knocked and waited and knocked again, assured by the man across the hall that Edward was in there, and finally I roused him, and after a few minutes talk, he got out of bed and dressed and we walked down to Queen Street and found a Turkish restaurant where Edward told me a little about the Turkish language and bickered amiably with the waiter over the distinction between Turkish and Lebanese food.

Now, two days later, I knocked and woke him and asked, too quickly perhaps, if he wanted to go out somewhere. No, he said, he was sleeping. If he got up, his sleep would be spoiled. So I closed the door and left him there. I never saw him again.

The last time I saw Robert Finch was on Hoskin Avenue, near Massey College, where I believe he maintained some connection after his retirement. This would have been in the early nineteen-eighties, and Finch, born in 1900, the same age as the century. He was, as always, perfectly dressed in a three-piece suit of excellent cut and quality—blue is what I remember—with a black homburg. I believe he was carrying a walking-stick, but his gait was firm and not slow. I saw the familiar figure coming toward me, that sunlit afternoon, and I stopped and spoke, introduced myself, and he was friendly and collected and remarked that he often saw things of mine in print, and said to himself, "Oh yes, there's something by David." We wished each other well and went on our way.

That I feel a connection between these two poets is partly historical accident. I met both of them at University College in the nineteen-fifties, but there is more to it than that. On the surface, they were very unlike, Lacey unkempt, disorderly, alcoholic, openly even boastfully homosexual, more than once in jail, Finch a very old-

8

fashioned kind of gentleman, an accomplished practitioner of at least three arts, at home in the university, a lifelong bachelor, his private life private, though there are reticent suggestions in his first book of sorrow for a lost love. Yet in Edward's letters to Henry Beissel he often mentions Robert Finch. He wrote from Bangkok in 1986, having seen a copy of the *Globe and Mail* in which a new book by Finch was mentioned, wondering if the man was still alive or if this was a posthumous work. He refers to Finch as his "old professor and mentor." In another letter there's a vignette that catches something of the character of the two men, a story about Finch advising Edward that one must keep hard at work to avoid the despair that was Edward's pursuer as he raced from country to country of the third world.

Let me look back at the University of Toronto in the years of the late nineteen-fifties. It is one of the conventions of recent history that the decade before 1960 was a period of stultifying mediocrity, yet the teachers at the university in those years included Northrop Frye and Marshall McLuhan and the students Margaret Atwood and a number of others who if a little less celebrated were equally part of the rapid expansion of Canadian writing a few years later. No doubt Toronto was the hard grey city Edward Lacey loved to hate, but you could find Timothy Findley and Glenn Gould there.

I believe it was in my first year as an undergraduate that I was taught French literature by Robert Finch. He was not what would now be called a charismatic teacher, but he was precise and fluent. Having myself been a teacher and abandoned it, having read a good deal of Finch's poetry, I can see the impossibility of such a man being found out by first-year students. Still, I had never in my life seen anyone dress that way, and I suppose that taught me something. Finch had a slight limp for a while,

9

and the rather baroque explanation current at University College was that while travelling in France he had become infected by a disease otherwise unknown since the middle ages. Which may not have been true, but was appropriate.

Perhaps Finch only taught us for half the year. Certainly my memories of the class are fragmentary, yet somehow I remained on friendly terms with him, and a couple of years later when I had won an undergraduate literary award, he asked to see the work I'd written and offered some kindly praise of a one-act play. I own a copy of his first book of poetry, published in 1946, which I got for 50¢ at the Oxford Press annual booksale. I never thought to ask him to sign it, but what I wrote was probably influenced by its sonnets and rhymed quatrains.

Somewhere in the distance, of course, Irving Layton was writing a very different kind of poetry, searching for prophetic splendour. Slaughtering monsters and bringing home the bleeding meat.

Perhaps all lives are heroic, but each in its own way. Certainly Robert Finch seems to have taken his own advice about hard work. As a young man he was a keyboard player accomplished enough to study with Wanda Landowska. An obituary reported that at the age of 94, he gave a private concert for friends. Myrtle Guerrero, the wife of Glenn Gould's teacher Alberto Guerrero, told a friend that she suspected that one of the pieces on a recent recording, said to be a duet played by Guerrero and Gould, might, in fact, be a duet that she had played with Robert Finch. True or not, it gives a sense of the man's abilities. I never heard Finch play, but I did once long ago see an exhibition of his paintings, rather silent landscapes composed of areas of flat colour, lyric but muted. Reticent, polished, a little haunted.

In 1958 I became one of the editors of the University College literary magazine, the *Undergrad*. The college had a fund that provided awards for undergraduate writing, and the winners of this contest were offered to the *Undergrad* for publication. One of the winners was someone named E. A. Lacey, for a group of translations from the eighteenth-century poet André Chénier. These translations are impressive even now, cleverly rhymed, metrical without being forced or laboured. I'm not sure that I knew then just how good they were, though we published them.

I can't place my first meeting with Edward but I do remember that by the next year it fell to me to try to persuade him to give us something new to publish. At first he said no, but finally agreed that we could publish a few things under a pseudonym. The one he chose was NBC. He suggested that apart from the television network, it might stand for Nellie Blythe Carr. One of the poems was called "Doctor Death."

"Incurable," says Doctor Death
Of this disease of drawing breath;
"I can prescribe an opiate, faith,
A purgative, hate, a palliative, hope,
And my old secret cure-all, rope."

That epigram was typical in both its wit and polish and its essential despair. One might say that it was the premature and unearned despair of an undergraduate except that it was at the core of Edward's personality, so far as I can see, for the rest of his life. As was the ambivalence about publication. He had the common desire for what he had written to be read but alongside that a need for privacy or concealment. Henry Beissel has explained how Edward insisted that his reviews in *EDGE* be presented under his own name with a note claiming that this was a pseudonym. Just his kind of joke.

I think it was in 1958 that Edward got thrown out of

the University College men's residence. Male undergrad-
uates were expected to show a certain amount of bravado
and rebelliousness, but Edward managed to do this, as
he did everything, in his own way. The residence had a
dining-hall attached, with student waiters and a student
headwaiter, a man with a certain ponderously serious
manner about him. On one occasion Edward, having had
one dinner, went back for another. (Or it may have been a
second dessert; I have most of this story at second hand.)
The headwaiter told him he mustn't take the second
helping, and Edward was defiant. This led to some kind of
trial before the residence disciplinary committee, known
—how very English and how very pretentious—as the
Caput.

This august body decided that Edward should be deprived of his food privileges for a period of time—one
week or two, I believe. This put Edward on his mettle,
and he replied by writing to all his professors—he was at
this time a senior student in languages and an outstand-
ingly brilliant one—to say that since he had been deprived
of his food privileges, he would be too weak to attend
classes and would have to languish in his room until his
period of enforced starvation was over.

This put the cat among the pigeons. The student newspaper became involved, and there were many late-night
meetings over the issue. It was a perfect example of his
inventive malice. A year later he came close to being
refused his degree when, though no longer living in the
residence, he drunkenly assaulted one of the residence
dons, pounding him on the chest and calling him a prick.
He explained to me that since everyone called the man a
prick behind his back, he thought it was time someone
said it to his face.

He was a loony and a troublemaker, but his brilliance
and thoughtfulness were undeniable. Though we weren't

12

close friends, he would now and then appear at the door of my room in the residence late at night to talk for a while. One of the things we had in common was a liking for minor poets. You could get at them, somehow, weren't held off by walls of historical piety. Edward appeared to remember every line of poetry he'd ever read, and he didn't quote to show off, simply to make a point. Alternately he would express malicious intentions toward his best friends or tell me stories about his war with a West Indian student who claimed to have a gun and was planning to shoot him.

I'm not around universities much these days, but I have the impression that they are increasingly institutions dominated by rules and procedures, and that there is probably less tolerance for eccentricity than there was in the supposedly dim and grim fifties. That was before universities became important and rich. I believe that for a while, Robert Finch, a man of middle age, a cultivated artist and poet, was one of the dons in that same men's residence, that is, he got free room and board and perhaps a small stipend for being responsible for keeping one residence house in order. I assume he needed the money. University teachers weren't paid much, but they were given a different kind of respect than is likely to be the case now. Decisions were made in private, and some of them may not have been absolutely fair, but Edward Lacey was respected for his astonishing abilities. Allowances were made.

In one of his letters to Henry Beissel—which were published just after his death under the title *A Magic Prison*—wondering whether he might or might not stay in Brazil, Edward Lacey writes: "I am mindful of Finch's injunction—'Think of each house you live in as a tent/ that holds you insecure from wear and tear/ and do not let its neighbourhood grow dear/ and never call its welcome

13

permanent,' etc. No sooner have I begun to think of the possibility of putting down roots in the places where I've lived, than events have begun to occur which would make it impossible to do so."

There he was, in Brazil, in 1969, quoting Robert Finch from memory and finding in the words an expression of his own feelings. Finch, who was born in Long Island, studied at University College, came back there in 1928 and stayed to teach there for the next 40 years, was certainly not a wanderer in the way Lacey was. Yet even when honoured by the university, he gave an impression of solitude—a solitude among friends. Neither poet is much read these days, I expect. They are not a part of the conventional story of Canadian writing. That's one link between the two of them, but I think there's more than that. What I'm trying to say has something to do with distance, self-possession, the lives of men who practiced their art with great concentration and mostly didn't get their names in the newspapers. Something to do with a verbal modesty, polish, a quality of tone. Though Lacey was homosexual and came to appreciate the support of the gay community, he was still a solitary. Finch and Lacey both write like men who were alone with words. There is a stillness, an absence.

Then in the summer of 1995, only a few days apart, they both died, and the past grew vivid in the light of that coincidence. I imagine one of those Albert Franck paintings of Toronto streets—that old Toronto of brick and wooden porches, those poignant windows in the secret houses. Winter and silence. Someone has just vanished around a corner or through a door, and I almost know who it is.

Presences

"I never wanted to be a butcher," Roy would say.

We would be standing around with nothing important to do, Roy and I talking a bit, old George Swan sometimes part of the conversation, more often not. The store where we worked was almost like two stores, the meat and vegetables on our side, and beyond an archway, almost cut off from us, the groceries, with an office and storerooms behind. There was something isolated, almost private, about our half of the store, even though its plate-glass windows faced the wide main street of Niagara-on-the-Lake.

When I remember it now, it seems to me that I heard Roy's story often, but perhaps it was just that kind of story, with the sound of something that had been told many times, to himself and to a few of the customers who were his friends, some who had been coming to the store for twenty years, who knew him from before the second war and his time in the army.

He would have liked to be a gardener and had some vague, half-formed plan that someday he would leave the butcher shop and work with flowers, growing things. I can't remember how or where this was to happen, but that hardly mattered, since the story was told for comfort, something to help him get through the day-by-day of work he hated.

We didn't have much time to talk most days, but I worked in the store part-time for several years, summers, weekends, sometimes after school, so the spare seconds and minutes added up to hours of conversation. I remember Roy leaning his big body against the back of the meat counter and looking past me with the mild eyes, the sweet clean slow manner of Jersey cattle and telling me things, telling me things, a bit here, a bit there, that added up to his steady self.

His car was a 1935 Packard, which he was still driving in the early fifties, a big square car that took him to work in the morning and home at night, and every Wednesday evening (we got Wednesday afternoon off) could be seen parked in front of the town movie, and in summer took its longest excursion, six or seven miles (each Sunday) to a park where there was a weekly band concert.

The car didn't last forever, not even the short forever of the years that I worked there. Looking back, it seems to me that one day Roy went out and got in the car, and it wouldn't start, and like a horse that won't get up, it was taken away and replaced by a year-old green Pontiac. Perhaps it didn't happen that way, but the car was replaced, and the green Pontiac appeared in all the places where the old Packard had been seen.

It must have been around that time that the girl came to work there, for in my memory she is connected with the new car.

There was Roy's brother too, a presence on a bicycle here and there on the streets of the town. Robert had no steady work, but he did odd jobs. He may have been dim or a bit mad, but he was a presence in Roy's life, not a family skeleton exactly (no kind of skeleton at all but like his brother a slow fat man), but I imagined him lying down a great deal, smiling, not exactly seeing Roy enter the house and leave it, but aware as a presence is aware of the person it is presenting itself to.

"I never wanted to be a butcher," Roy would say and tell the story of how, when he was perhaps thirteen, his father decided he must be set to work and took him to a butcher shop (because it was the closest place perhaps, there was never a reason given) and told them to make a butcher of him.

"I always thought that was wrong," he said, not so much a grievance as a statement of principle, one that had taken him some time to be sure of, one that he was humble enough not to force on you, but a statement of principle all the same.

What Roy liked best in this job he didn't like was waiting on customers, passing the time of day, giving the best cuts, the leanest hamburger to his favourites, proud that the store sold only the highest quality meat, that we didn't grind the hamburger in advance so it was always fresh and everyone could see it was not adulterated.

My jobs were various. The earliest were slicing bacon and cutting up scraps for hamburger, and these remained occasional responsibilities, but as I learned more, I took up new jobs, filling orders, serving a few customers, even such exotic activities as trying to drive the wild cat out of the basement or making a new crock of brine.

The corned beef was a matter for occasional angry disputes between Roy and George, but everything was at some time or another, for their disagreement was like God whose centre is everywhere and circumference nowhere. It had probably been that way for years. Soon after my arrival in the butcher shop, I became a territory up for grabs, for I was hired by the manager who supervised the whole of the double store, hired on the assumption that they could use someone young and cheap, and I started on neutral ground working at the vegetable counter, but when that was finished, there were bitter disputes about whether I should help George cut hamburger or help Roy prepare the orders for delivery, but after a while I got settled into a sequence of duties, and somehow everything got done.

George had his stories too, of course. He was old enough and (we suspected) rich enough to retire, but he liked the work and liked the money and showed no sign of being close to the day when he would stop liking either.

("Those others," George would say to me under his breath, "they're not butchers. They've never killed an animal. They're just meat cutters."

"What if a customer saw him doing that?" Roy would say to me after George had blown from his nose a great cascade of mucus, snapping it down between his fingers to the sawdust floor of the meat cooler.)

George had a metal plate in his head that foretold the coming of rain. It did this by making his head ache and his temper, which was never good, became worse than ever. At some time in the past, he had owned his own store, but a horse had run wild in a local horse show, and he had been thrown from a buggy and had fallen on his head. He sold his store and was unable to work for some time, finally going back to cutting meat in someone else's store, his ability to foretell the weather (of which he was publicly proud) a small and painful compensation for what he had lost.

He too had a car, and its path, like the path of Roy's car, was regular. We would see it only on Saturday nights when the store stayed open until nine o'clock. The other days of the week, George arrived by bus in the morning and left by bus when the store closed, but on Saturday night his wife would come for him in a big black Buick, which she would park outside the plate-glass window of the butcher shop. She would wait there for George to finish, and I never once saw her get out of the car or come into the store.

George liked to tell me about his wife's driving. She drove, he always said, at exactly the speed limit, 50 miles an hour, not one mile over and not one mile under. I'd think of that as I saw the black car taking him away each Saturday night.

Old George was a shorter, even fatter man than Roy, and his very belly was aggressive, and especially on days when his head was bad, he would walk, quick and angry, down the narrow alley behind the meat counter with a large chunk of beef and a butcher knife resting on that big belly, defying anyone to step in front of him. He didn't dare run into Roy, but no-one else was safe, and hours of muttering followed each collision.

Then there was the morning of the rat: I was often a few minutes late for work, and when I walked in that morning, I could hear Roy's angry voice from the back corner by our sink and could see George working in hostile isolation on the wooden chopping-block. I put on my apron and walked back to the sink where Roy told me what had happened. A rat had been caught by the tail in one of the traps I had set, and George, who found it, dealt with the thing by holding it on the wooden block where the meat was cut and chopping off its head with a meat cleaver. Now Roy was furiously disinfecting everything in the store.

Angry rumbling went on, the rat one day, something else the next, some days cheerful enough until there would be an exchange over the hamburger, Roy picking out the leanest pieces leaving George to sell the fat (which he objected to in principle but was happy enough to do in practice, for he would be greedy not just on his own behalf, but on behalf of the store as well.)

Then the girl came, to work part-time on the vegetable counter. I was not fond of her, though we got on well enough. She was a member of the evangelical Mennonite Brethren. I had seen them once on a Sunday morning baptising adults at the public beach, the minister's black gown floating out around him as he stood waist deep in the water. The girl had the bright hypocritical sunniness and the unctuous solicitude that can go with a certain kind of evangelical piety. She was small and neatly enough put together that if someone else had lived in her body, I might have found it attractive. As it was, it provoked only a cold curiosity. I shared the amusement of the other boys in the store when one of them set her to looking through the cobs of corn for corn-holers, encouraging her to repeat the phrase out loud.

But there she was, day after day, like all of us, like the store fixtures, something the customers, passing like time, passed by.

A tableau from the days after she came: Roy is leaning heavily on the vegetable counter near the girl, he dressed all in white, jacket and huge apron, she in a dress or skirt and blouse (sometimes a short-sleeved blouse so that when she reached up I could see the brown hair under her arm) and a white apron over it, George facing away from the two of them, behind the meat counter, cutting away at a piece of meat, his fat face blank and enraged.

Roy told the girl all his stories. He carried out the heavy crates of vegetables for her. He drove her home sometimes when the weather was bad or on Saturday nights after we had worked late. In the tableau in my memory, the two of them are always there in that corner, and the girl smiles at Roy, and he tells her all his stories. George had often said that he did more than his share of the work in the butcher shop, and after the girl came and Roy began to spend time talking to her, George's anger increased, crowding his pained head with storms.

I missed the final fight. One day I came up from cleaning the basement, and there was no-one behind the meat counter but the store manager. Everyone was working with ominous concentration, and it was a few minutes until I learned that George and Roy were out in the back storeroom with the owner. Neither one appeared as the afternoon went on, ended, and we closed the store. The next morning George wasn't at work, and everyone knew, without a word said, that he wouldn't be back, and it was

20

possible to miss him, crude and vicious and blundering as he was. His absence had, at first, some of the force of his presence.

No doubt Roy talked to the girl a little less often, for a while at least. He had won, but he never said a word to me to suggest that he rejoiced in his victory which anyway only lasted for a few weeks until the arrival of a new butcher. He too was fat, this new butcher, fat and loud and effeminate and crude, poking, prodding, laughing. "How's your dink?" he would say pretty much every time he went by. Every five minutes, it seemed, he went away for a long conference with the owner and the store manager. Later the two of them would talk to Roy.

Soon the meat cooler held a chunk of the carcass of an old bull, and pieces were added to our hamburger to give it more colour, to make it look leaner. We ground the hamburger ahead of time now and scooped out a handful to weigh to the customer's request. We got a machine that could turn almost anything into minute steak, chopping the meat apart and patching it together all in one operation. Things happened fast now, and kept happening. Roy complained a bit, but this was part of his victory, and he had to live with it.

Sometime during all this, the girl got engaged. Her boyfriend began to meet her after work, and we all got to know him, but Roy especially, since Roy was her friend. When she married, Roy was the only one from the store who was at the wedding. She married and left, and soon I left too. Roy stayed, of course, waiting for the day when he would learn how to move on. I went off to university, but when I was back in town, I'd drop in at the store, and Roy and I would talk a bit, old friends who no longer had anything to say.

My parents stayed in Niagara, and it was my mother who told me Roy was dead. Suffered a heart attack, lingered on in hospital and then died. He hadn't, she said, appeared to care all that much about living. I would like to think I gave Roy more than a moment's thought. In another century I suppose I would have offered a prayer for his soul.

A Short History of Food

My grandfather wouldn't eat spaghetti—Heinz, from the tin, that is, what spaghetti meant in 1950. He was a Yorkshireman, and though he had emigrated, he maintained his insularity in this matter. Last month, out to dinner with my daughter and her husband to celebrate her birthday, I ordered ravioli stuffed with duck, a black-bean soup and a main course of scallops with a stuffed and baked red onion.

There are many ways to look at our passage through life, and one day it came to me that what I have eaten or cooked over the years is one measure of the changes the world has gone through. It is a truism that while change is a constant, the speed of change has increased in the twentieth century. You could quote statistics. Part of the metamorphosis of every life is personal and unique, or at least we hope so. The grandfather who wouldn't eat spaghetti was a working-class English boy who grew up without decent shoes. When he was given some, his wicked stepmother took them away and gave them to her son, his half-brother. He was apprenticed to a painter and paperhanger, married a daughter of the family and worked at the trade all his life, except in the bad periods when there was no work and they had to get along without or go on relief. A candidate for escape, I got an education, and learned to live by my wits. I maintained some old loyalties. My idea of the upper middle class was people who fed their children, sent them to bed and then sat down to dinner. Didn't do that.

One of the first books ever printed was a cookbook, and there is a vast literature of writing about food. I think it was in 1961 that *The Observer*, one of the English quality Sunday papers, had a large feature on restaurants and a week later printed a letter from a reader who objected to a serious newspaper "giving pride of place to an article on food." I'm not altogether sure why that stuck in my mind, but it suggests that a fearsome English puritanism was still hanging on and quick to attack cavalier indulgence. That was a battle with a long history: *Dost thou think because thou art virtuous, there shall be no more cakes and ale?* A little more than a decade after the exchange in *The Observer*, Oberon Press, who published my poetry, brought out *Where to Eat in Canada*, which became an annual bestseller. Now stylish restaurants are one of the features of city culture everywhere in the western world. Newspapers and magazines all have restaurant reviews, mostly written in a knowing style full of overfine distinctions.

Back in the years when my grandfather was resisting Heinz spaghetti, going out to a restaurant meant a hot beef sandwich at the United Cigar Store, cold roast beef laid between two slices of cold white bread and covered with thick brown gravy, the whole accompanied by peas from a tin and maybe french fries, and as I write that, the memory is making my mouth water. Though the United Cigar Stores are gone, you can still get a hot beef sandwich, or hot chicken or hot turkey, but the restaurants that serve it will never get listed in expensive magazines. It's already years since radicchio became a source of jokes about the upwardly mobile and their snobberies.

I belong to the generation of men who reacted to the new demand for fairness by learning to cook, and I've learned that food is far more than what we use to satisfy an appetite. It's the core of our sociability, and a symbolic language that relates us to the world. Prison riots are often prompted by complaints about the food. To live in the twentieth century is to live in a world of labels, and even the most old-fashioned men, macho brutes to the core, will have their favourite beer and cigarettes or scotch and cigars.

Where to start? Cereal: All Bran and Shredded Wheat. This was in the days before cereal was covered with sugar. (I'll get to sugar later.) Now what I remember about those two cereals has nothing to do with eating them. They both had free cards. The great food corporations were continuing the expansion begun in the nineteen-twenties, and food was tied to advertising and the importance of brand names. Shredded Wheat had box-grey cards with pictures to be coloured, while All Bran had brightly coloured cards that could be collected, traded, or flipped in a game of skill in which you tried to match the other guy's card, face up or down. The cards came in series, wild animals, planes, the guns and other weapons currently in use in the second world war, probably others. Not hockey players, I think, though at one stage I got autographed photographs by saving labels from Beehive Corn Syrup, shining black-and-white prints of Syl Apps, Ted Kennedy, Turk Broda, the heroes of the Toronto Maple Leafs, but that was later. I collected the cards from All Bran when we still lived in Toronto; in those days I got much of my information about the world from those cereal cards—for years I thought there was a monkey called the orange utang—and the rest from radio and the Toronto *Star*.

In 1948, we moved from Toronto to Niagara-on-the-Lake. This was fruit-growing country, and behind the barn where my father worked was a large garden with a peach tree that never amounted to much, bushes bearing raspberries, red currants and blackcurrants, and more exotic still, a quince tree. The quince, apparently, is a native of Iran and Turkey, and was once widely grown in the northeastern United States, but lost favour. At least one year, my mother used the fruit to make a clear jelly with a beautiful colour somewhere between pink and yellow, very

25

close to the theatrical lighting gel that used to be called bastard amber. I don't remember much home canning before we moved, but now every summer, she did down the local fruits, and in the tiny cellar under the kitchen, there were shelves with jars of preserves to carry us through the winter.

Niagara was enough to make an epicure of anyone, the rows of blossoming trees in the spring, the sequence of crops, strawberries, cherries, peaches, pears, grapes, the brightly feathered ring-necked pheasants living in the orchards and hedgerows, flying up with a clucking and clatter of wings when my dog found them. They make fine wines there now, where in my day there were only wines that were given nicknames like Bright's Disease. One time I picked strawberries and another cherries for local farmers, but I was young and lazy, no match for the itinerant pickers who did most of the work.

My mother was a traditional sort of cook who liked feeding people. Years before, when we lived in Hamilton, we had a boarder for a while, and in Toronto, young men who worked for my father in his small furniture business were given lunch. It was the days of food from tins—one version of the modern—and we ate a lot of it, though we also had home-made pickles, and local vegetables in season, asparagus, vegetable marrow, butternut squash. Just up the road, in Virgil, Miss Field and her brother ran a small farm and market garden with a little stand on the highway, and it was from them we learned about corn. They wouldn't sell you corn unless it had been picked that very day, and when my father, who repaired furniture in the barn behind the house, was ready for his lunch, he or my mother would jump in the car and drive the five or ten minutes out to Virgil and come back with corn that had been picked only an hour or so before. Now there are hybrids with higher levels of sugar so that it takes longer for sweet corn to break down into the starchy sludge that must be heavily coated with butter and salt, but before these hybrids were developed, you had to grow corn or live near someone who did to understand the sweetness of the vegetable when it was new.

There were fishermen working the lake in those days, taking pickerel, whitefish, the occasional sturgeon, but my mother wasn't fond of fish, which offended her fastidious nose, so even though our neighbour Franklin Currie was a fisherman—I could recognize his boat docked at the slip with the boats of the other local men—I wasn't fed on the fish they brought in and sold at a wholesaler's shack on a beach near the mouth of the river. Perhaps that's just as well; even then, I think, the Love Canal was beginning to leach chemical effluents into the river. In a few years the fish were gone.

In my teens, I got my first job, in a store just across the main street, working summers and on weekends all through high school, and if I didn't already know about food, I couldn't have spent all those years in the butcher shop without learning. Roy, the meat manager, had been a cook in the army. I'm not convinced army cooking was the best training for advising the women who came to the counter to buy meat from him, but he at least had some awareness of where the meat went after he sold it. George, the other butcher, didn't much care.

Under the store, there was a basement, damp and ancient, where wild cats were sometimes seen. I might be sent down there to dump a 100-pound sack of potatoes into a wooden bin, then take them out with a big metal scoop and put them into five or ten-pound bags on an old scale with a steel plate on the floor and a weighted beam above, or I would have to turn over the 50-pound cheeses that were left there to age. The cheeses came in round wooden boxes, and after a few months in the basement,

27

someone would cut a round perhaps four inches high by drawing through the column of cheese a wire on handles—exactly the technique you would use to garrote someone—and then the round of cheese was brought up and placed on a device with a hinged handle that was drawn down to cut it into triangular slices. Among schoolboys, farting was known as cutting the cheese, and there was a powerful smell from that aged cheddar. The store had some small notoriety for its fine old cheese, well aged in the basement, but the whole truth was that the cheese was produced by J. M. Schneider, the meat packers, and the original ageing was done by them, though the store bought only April and September cheeses, those being for some reason the best or most flavourful, and it may well be that the musty basement had some significant moulds to add. I had been brought up on Kraft Velveeta, but now, following my father, I developed a taste for the rank old cheddar.

Upstairs, the meat and vegetables were stored in walk-in coolers, and another of my responsibilities was the brine in which the corned beef was pickled. This was made in a waist-high crock that stood in the vegetable cooler. Beef brisket, including pieces that had begun to look a little stale, was thrown into the brine to be preserved there. Beef tongues, with their thick root and long lolling tip were pickled as well. Now and then the brine would be dumped and a new pickle prepared, bags of salt and a little saltpetre, potassium nitrate I fetched from the drugstore up the street. I was never quite sure whether this was perfectly legal; there was a well-known tale about how the army added saltpetre to soldiers' food to inhibit their sexual desire or performance. Traditional butchers had their own ways. Someone local was said to have been charged with adding embalming fluid to his cuts of meat to help keep them from going off, and certainly George threw into the pickle pieces of brisket that were in no very good state of health.

Not long before, my parents had bought their first refrigerator. When we lived in Toronto, we had an icebox, and either Lake Simcoe Ice or Belle Ewart Ice would come once or twice a week—you put a card in the window to indicate that you wanted ice, and what size, 25 pounds or 50—and ice would be put in the top of it. Frozen food had been around in some form since the nineteen-thirties, but I don't remember anyone buying frozen fish until after we had moved to Niagara. By the time I went to work in the store, there were commercial freezers everywhere, and when you put up an order for delivery, you would add a slip of paper telling Donnie, who drove the truck and did the deliveries, to put in one or another kind of frozen food when he was loading up. Donnie had come to the store as a clerk and been promoted to driver. He came to a sad end, years after I left, but that's another story, as one says, not wanting to tell it.

I wasn't a butcher, but I became familiar with most cuts of meat and achieved some skill with a knife and a cleaver. Chickens came with feet and head still attached, all the guts still within, and after the bird was weighed, you chopped off the head and feet with a cleaver, cut through the boneless cavity between the legs, carefully around the anus, put in your hand and yanked out the inner parts. Heart, liver, neck and gizzard were tucked back inside, and the rest rolled up in brown paper and dropped into one of the bushel baskets under the heavy wooden cutting blocks. To eviscerate a boiling fowl was a messy job, since these old hens were full of eggs in various stages of development. If I was ever going to be squeamish, I was cured by having to be able to come back to work after a big meal and haul the guts out of a boiling fowl.

Things I learned to eat: the jellied tongue that came

29

in metal tins with flat sides and bottom and rounded ends, a piece of cardboard on top, and which was sliced on one of the mechanical slicers, at first one that was cranked by hand, later an electric one; head cheese, which might or might not have been made from brains; an occasional taste of lean raw beef. We weren't supposed to eat any of these things, but I was a boy in his teens, and it was hard to resist. Roy had explained early on that pork might be afflicted with trichonosis and must be well cooked, but I learned to like raw beef. Some of the rich Americans bought steaks two inches thick to barbecue, and it seemed unlikely that the heat would ever get to the middle. Beef rare and beef raw weren't that far apart.

The store also sold things my family didn't eat. Garlic and eggplant, the first smelly and distasteful, something for loud and probably none-too-clean Italians, and the second exotic. I don't think my mother would have known what to do with it. There were also, because the store had a rich clientele, at least in the summer, strange things like tins of turtle soup, jars of caviar, foods for the well-to-do.

By the end of high school, it was all familiar, the coolers hung with quarters of beef, the bright ruby red of the meat, the smooth ivory gloss of the fat, the headless carcasses of lamb waiting to be split, the chickens hanging upside down by their feet, a slightly raffish, pixilated look on their dead inverted faces with bright red combs; in the refrigerated counter lay the trays of oven roasts and pot roasts, brisket flat and rolled, and across the room stood the long vegetable cooler with imported lettuces at one end and imported oranges at the other.

That was the old world, but a new world was coming. In *Paradox of Plenty: A Social History of Eating in America*, Harvey Levenstein defines in a sentence, the change that came about at the end of my youth: "the national community of shared values that had persisted for twenty-odd years after World War II—years in which even those in the highest economic and social brackets appeared to share the straightforward national food tastes—seemed to break down, as food again became an important sign of distinction." It was around the end of high school that I had my first experience of pizza. That sounds absurd now, when pizza has conquered the planet, but the closest thing to fast food I can remember before that, apart from the cafeterias in department stores, was a red hot at The Honey Dew, Honey Dew itself being a sweet acidy orange drink that was the house specialty. A red hot at the Honey Dew: it sounds now like the punchline of an old-fashioned dirty joke.

Pizza: in New York State, which was just a few minutes away across the Niagara River, you could drink beer, weak American beer, when you were eighteen, which meant you could try at seventeen or earlier. I went to high school miles from home in Niagara Falls, after a trip on the school bus, every day for five years, and the bridge to the US wasn't as easily accessible to me as it was to my friends who lived in the city, but I heard about Peewee's Pizzeria and eventually made the fabulous voyage across the river. In one of my last summers in Niagara, I spent every evening on the golf course with two friends. We would stand on the ninth green when it was almost dark, putting for pennies, and then we would drive to Niagara Falls, NY and go to Peewee's for pizza and beer. Ah, the good life.

An encyclopedia tells me that the first pizzeria was opened in New York City in 1905, and that the pizza boom in the US began after the second war. Soon there was scarcely a hamlet without a pizzeria. Well, in the nineteen-fifties it was all new to me, though ten years later, the pizza epidemic had spread to Canada as well, and twenty years after that we entered the era of gourmet pizza—fine cheeses on a thin crust baked in a wood oven.

People define themselves by their pizza toppings. I draw the line at pineapple.

Pizza everywhere by the early nineteen-sixties, and at home spaghetti and chili; everyone had a recipe for chili con carne or spaghetti sauce, spicy mush that could be cooked and eaten in quantity. We were all bohemians now. In the meantime, I had lived for two years in England. Which meant on the one hand a meal in a large restaurant in Chester, grey damp tasteless lamb, a mush of potatoes, and peas with the green colour running out onto the plate, and on the other hand, the wonderful cheeses of Cheshire, Caerphilly, Wensleydale. There is no-one quite like the English.

I said I'd get back to sugar. In her forties, my mother was discovered to be diabetic, and she spent the rest of her life taking insulin, though not being as careful about her diet as she might have been. All the same, she was 87 when she died. In the meantime I was sent to drink a jug of vile sugar water and told that I was on the fringes of the disease, and so I began to train myself to do without sugar and to become aware of the amount most people eat. Later my daughter Maggie, fanatic about everything in her youth, began a regimen of pure eating that was the first step toward her later anorexia. She has written essays about food and love and her fascination with hunger, and there is nothing for me to add to them, except to say that I was changed by it all. When she stopped eating sugar, we began to read the labels on food. If it had been put in a tin or package, there was sugar in it. There are exceptions to that rule, but not many. Probably there was a time when the concentrated calories of sugar were a positive and necessary addition to the diet of the undernourished, but by now, it is merely the most commonplace north American addiction.

How is it that styles change? Regency becomes Victorian, but surely not because of the young queen. It's as if some new ideas are like a highly contagious disease, once introduced, they run rampant. Now suddenly there was a plague of vegetarianism, talk of the macrobiotic diet among young people as pale as mushrooms raised in the dark. In Toronto as a child I was aware of one couple, friends of my parents, who were vegetarians. They were quiet, rather delicate people, I think, though memory here is on the edge of invention. Certainly they had no children, and in some way I connected the two facts about them and saw their vegetarianism as part of some mysterious sexual incapacity. However the new vegetarianism was allied to the raunchy and high-minded melodrama of the antiwar movement. Nutritionists like Adele Davis were everywhere. Diet was a code, that allowed subtle distinctions among the various tribes. Everyone was quoting the slogan, You Are What You Eat, a punchier version of the aphorism of the French gastronome Brillat-Savarin first published in 1826: "Tell me what you eat: I will tell you what you are."

When Maggie got interested in food, she brought home books about food and reading them, I began to think about it all. The unexamined meal was not worth eating. In restaurants I poked at things to see how they had been made. I tried using recipes in their original form. It's not surprising that after spending hours every day sitting at a table arranging words, I liked to cut and chop, though I brought the same mind to both activities. Always the sort of poet who found it hard to resist difficult rhymed and metrical forms, I started to think of cooking the same way, good meals from fresh and simple ingredients, vegetables in season. To cook the way Hemingway wrote prose, and just as in writing, it is easy to slip from brilliant clarity to baroque mannerism, as Hemingway did. Someone gave me a copy of the *Larousse Gastronomique*, and

33

I bought reprints of old cookbooks. I became fanatic, bad-tempered and tiresome.

Julia Child, The Galloping Gourmet, Bruno Gerussi in the kitchen: television, like magazines, was fascinated by food. Stylish food once meant a version of French cooking. When I was at university, there was a Toronto restaurant called La Chaumière that was the acme of elegance, but as more people travelled, and as the American empire expanded, new nationalities became the source of new tastes—Japanese, Szechuan, Mexican, Thai, and on and on across the globe. Styles in food changed as quickly as styles in clothing, and perhaps for some of the same reasons. Style, in fact, became an obsession, as kitchens began to be equipped with steamers, woks, blenders and even more complicated machines. The pursuit of novelty drove food writers to praise ever more exotic ingredients.

Now our lives are dominated by technology and consciousness, sociologists are quick to note and analyze the changes in the ways things happen. To an extent, the thinkers can explain why the style of our time is a passionate concern with style, but there are mysteries as well. Why *did* Regency make way for Victorian?

Many years ago when I worked at the CBC and spent the weeknights alone in an apartment, my regular dinner was half a pound of sausage and a pot of frozen peas. I still adore a slap-up breakfast at a greasy spoon, but I have braids of home-grown garlic hanging in the kitchen. At local farmers' markets I meet those who are most like me. Looking back at what I have used to nourish my flesh, I can't be unaware that I have followed the manners of my own time and class. See above, *passim*. How avoid it: to live outside the manners of your age requires eccentricity or an effort of will. We all like to think that we are original, but only a few have a talent for freedom, and great originality is perhaps a kind of madness.

34

Now the past grows longer, the future shorter, the distance of the echoes alters, and what we are left with is telling stories about what we saw as we got here. To believe that the past was better is sentimentality, but it is important to insist that the past was, and the weight of the specific is a defence against the commonplace. The seasons are still with us. Though it is accepted wisdom that by the nineteen-thirties improved food storage and transportation had ended the distinction of the seasons in North American diet, here in PEI, I still see little groups of labourers in the November fields pulling turnips from the ground, lopping the two ends and throwing them into a wooden crate. It may be that we must endure the technological paradise, but someone will buy and eat all those turnips this winter, there are leeks left in my garden, and the general store across the road still sells can of Heinz spaghetti, though I don't buy them. I'm with my grandfather on that.

Our Fathers Who Begat Us

I

The book is bound in black leather. The spine is torn, and the binding has dust deeply embedded. Opening it and turning the pages can make me sneeze, and even my not-very-sensitive nose catches the bitter smell of age and mould. On the front in embossed gold letters the name Mr. David Abbott, my maternal grandfather. I have written about my mother's family history, the fact that he wasn't my biological grandfather, but he was the grandfather I always knew, and the book came to me from my mother, an heirloom and a curiosity. On the title page a date is inserted in red ink, Feb. 6, 1909 and on the flyleaf an address, 724 Crawford Street, Toronto, Canada. My grandmother's family had immigrated to Canada from Leeds not long before that date. My great-grandfather, a painter and paperhanger, practised his trade from that house just to the west of Christie Pits, and my grandfather, who had been his apprentice, worked with him.

The title page reads *The Lyceum Manual, A Compendium of Physical, Moral and Spiritual Exercises For Use In Progressive Lyceums Connected with British Spiritualists' Societies.* My mother's family worshipped, if that is the word, at the Dovercourt Spiritualist Chapel, and David Abbott was a member of a male quartet that sang there. A tenor, I would think, from what I remember of his voice.

By the time she was in her teens, my mother was singing in the choir of what was, or became—this was just at the time of church union—the United Church in Uxbridge, a little town north of Toronto where she had found her first job, but in her childhood, she attended that spiritualist chapel where marching and calisthenics were part of the regular routine, something she found lively

36

enough to make the weekly routine of church less daunt-
ing than many children have found it.

*Two strokes of the bell calls the Officers to stand up, when they
quietly take their places at the head, behind the Guardian of
Groups, who leads the Lyceum in marching in single file, counter
marching, double ranks, chain march, etc. etc., the Conductor
reserving the guards at pleasure to assist in maintaining order.*

My mother was not a person who enjoyed recalling the
past, but she did remember that the leader was a large
woman, with one of those short, firm, northcountry names,
Stubbs, Camm, Thurll, one of those.

*In order to assume position for Calisthenics, it should be previ-
ously ascertained how many the hall will accommodate at full
arm's length across—let us say it will accommodate six; on the
conclusion of the marching the Lyceum falls into single file as
they march round the hall, the leading six take up their extended
position across the hall at sufficient distance from the rostrum and
face towards it; the seventh will lead the next six in front of
these, the thirteenth his six in front of these; and so on until all
are arranged in front of the rostrum, the least being in front.
The Calisthenic exercises are then gone through, led by the conductor.*

Sometime in the course of the program (so called in the
little book) my mother recalled that each child was to
offer a Pearl. Of wisdom, I suppose. My mother's favourite, which she found was readily acceptable, "Always do as
mother says."

There's much more I'd like to know about the family
history in the spiritualist movement. In their late years,
my grandparents moved to Niagara-on-the-Lake, where I
lived with my parents, and they attended the United
Church there. My grandfather officially joined the United
Church; I seem to remember that he was baptised in order
to do so. My grandmother didn't join, though I never
knew her reasons. She was a woman of some character, and

37

quite possibly she was still loyal to the doctrines of her youth.

Conductor—What is the chief principle of our system?

Lyceum—Harmony.

Conductor—What is its particular manifestation?

Lyceum—Music and singing, in which our unity of feeling and purpose is symbolized and expressed.

Conductor—What is the invariable accompaniment of our exertions.

Lyceum—Pleasure. That which is right is always delightful to the healthy spirit.

Whatever these people were, it is clear that they were not Christians, though they believed very firmly in the existence of the spirit and its eternal life.

Conductor—What is the spirit?

Lyceum—A self-conscious being in human form, manifesting affection and intelligence.

Conductor—What is its destiny?

Lyceum—Everlasting life and everlasting ascension through endless realms of thought and action.

These quotations are taken from the Golden Chain recitations, catechistic question-and-answer expositions of doctrine taken from an eclectic groups of sources, including Thomas Paine, Swedenborg, the Talmud, Wordsworth, Marcus Aurelius, the Bible, and the Spirits Speaking Through Mrs. Emma Hardinge-Britten. The whole has about it the air of the high-minded autodidact, of people who have found orthodox belief cramped and rigid and have set out to concoct something better. This is the world that produced the Quakers and later the Shakers, serious-minded eccentrics unable to tolerate orthodoxy, in rebellion against their betters in the established church. There is an odd mixture of credulity and respect for reason.

Conductor—Have the saints been martyrs?

Lyceum—Many have sealed their mission with their life, or great self-sacrifice.

Conductor—Are they numerous?

Lyceum—The Truth has thousands of such from Socrates to Bruno, from Galileo to Paine.

This suggests the attitudes of secular rationalists, those who put thought and science ahead of the authority of doctrine.

Conductor—Are there any women saints and martyrs?

Lyceum—A great number;—Aspasia, Cornelia, Hypatia, Joan of Arc, Florence Nightingale and Grace Darling.

I had to look up those classical references. In each case it is a powerful woman who was defamed by those around her. Hypatia in particular is an interesting figure, a beautiful Neoplatonist and mathematician, who was murdered by Christian monks. The spiritualists had an element of feminism alongside their respect for religious sceptics. Yet they were firmly attached to a belief in communication through mediums.

Conductor—What is a Medium?

Lyceum—A Medium is a person through whose organic structure departed spirits can communicate with people in this life.

The attitude to the spiritual realm is both complacent and rebellious. It seems to have been called the Summer Land, at least by some believers.

Sweet Summer Land! oh may I be
Prepar'd to view thy glories free.
Oh! may I be so free from guile
My soul may mirror back thy smile.

Another hymn nearby in the book, obviously to be sung to the tune of "The Battle Hymn of the Republic" is explicitly anti-Christian. "The Resurrection trumpet shall not wake us from the sod," it says, and "we need not ask Saint

39

Peter to be ready with his keys." There's a hint of political rebellion as well; "deepest thunders of Progression are now shaking tyrants' thrones."

All this reminds me of my grandfather's politics. He thought of himself as a communist of some sort—"The capitalists would call me a communist and the communists would call me a capitalist," he once said to me. He saw the Bolsheviks as corrupters of a purer communist doctrine. From the seventeenth century on, radical doctrines in religion and politics had been mixed in England, a ferment of rebellion that burst out in mystical enthusiasm or political action. Though Blake doesn't appear to be mentioned in the Lyceum Manual, I feel him close by.

Children were taught a strict egalitarianism.

Conductor—Treat all playmates as equals by right. <u>We are all brothers and sisters; and there is no high, no low, except in spiritual attainments.</u>

Be generous to make others happy, even with playthings; they are childhood's treasures.

The bud of generosity in the child will unfold into the flower of benevolence in the adult.

That underlined passage is the only one in the whole book to be given extra emphasis. Instead of the usual doctrine of good and bad, sinner and righteous, the world here is all one. The insistence on the survival of every soul takes the emphasis away from any idea of redemption, the separation of sheep and goats, and insists on eternity for all. The lack of the cruelty and rage that is often part of religious doctrine is striking.

Conductor—Never throw stones at passing travellers, nor at innocent beasts or birds.

Never call anyone by an unwelcome nickname.

Try, in every way you can, to make the world a good and pleasant place to yourself and others.

Laugh, frolic, dance, and be merry; but be ye also innocent.

40

Songs of Innocence: I'm reminded that they used to call Pelagianism the English heresy. There may be more than a hint of sentimentality, but it's all very decent, high-minded, even when it's comic.

This little song was chanted by a happy group of children from the Summer Land, and the lady medium who heard it was enabled to record both the words and the music.—Additional words by Miss E.C. Odiorne.

It's hard to say how much of this was in the air of my grandparents' life when I was born 30 years later. So far as I know the Dovercourt Spiritualist Chapel was long gone. I think I can fairly say that there was never a strong sense of orthodoxy, political or religious. I remember discussing politics with my grandfather, and the things he said about communism, he said to me one afternoon as we stood in my father's workshop.

It's not hard to make a case that by now all religious orthodoxy is vanishing. Ever more wishful sets of beliefs are arising—aliens, angels, Elvis sightings, channellings to other levels of being, a populist spirituality. More people, we are told, believe in flying saucers than believe in God. All these things seize on religious imagery while avoiding its intellectual or moral content. The poetry without the need to think what it might mean. Recently, an essay I was commissioned to write got reprinted in *The Canadian Unitarian* and I was sent a copy. UUs, these people call themselves, (Unitarians and Universalists), and their religion seems to be an attempt to keep the moral content of the old faith without doctrine or imagery. The little ceremonies they invent have about them the pallid pathos of the well-meaning.

To some extent all religious imagery is of its time and place. Those high-minded, self-educated working class Britons in the spiritualist chapels carved out what they could, eclectic and eager, turning their backs on sin to look toward some kind of egalitarian and universal bliss. The classless society that would be found on the other side, the mediums offering glimpses of that eternal joy.

My grandfather came out of that world. He was a kindly if irascible working man with little education, whose childhood was abusive even by the standards of Victorian England. He liked to read my comic-books. I own a set of Dickens in 22 volumes, the Popular Edition issued by Chapman and Hall in 1907 which, though they had little enough money, he bought as a gesture toward higher things. It would have to be Dickens of course, that inspired cockney, who had known poverty and whose religion was a mixture of sentimentality and simple decency. Perhaps my grandfather recognized his own childhood as Dickensian, but he had left all that behind in the dim narrow streets of Leeds. He was, I was told, very proud of his place in the Lyceum quartet at that chapel on Dovercourt Road, and of the Lyceum Manual with his name embossed in gold, which now lies on the table in front of me, smelling of the past, making me sneeze.

2

I was on the ferry to Nova Scotia when I was introduced to a woman who had trouble with my last name; when she realized that it was German, she was puzzled that I didn't speak the language. Her family was from PEI, which means that her ancestors were from the British Isles or were Acadian French. To her, Europeans were recent arrivals. I explained that my German forbears had come to Canada in the eighteen-forties, and as the ferry came ashore at Caribou, I thought for the first time that those German immigrants must have been among the earliest arrivals who weren't from France or some part of Great

42

Britain. Obvious enough, but a new idea to me.

A month or so later, I read *The Great Hunger*, Cecil Woodham-Smith's account of the Irish famine and emigration that took place after the potato crop was destroyed by blight. The Irish ships that arrived at Grosse Ile above Quebec were loaded with sick and famished men, women and children, many of whom were left to die on the island while others went on to spread disease through the cities of Eastern Canada and a few survived to settle or cross to the United States. There is an account by a cabin passenger on one of those doomed Irish boats of a very different kind of ship.

Whyte then witnessed the arrival of a shipload of German emigrants. The crowded vessel carried more than five hundred passengers, but there was no sickness and all were "neatly clad." The medical examination took place on deck, and "each comely fair-haired girl laughed as she passed the doctor to join a group of robust young men." As the vessel went up the river "the deck was covered with emigrants who were singing a charming hymn in whose beautiful harmony all took part." Throughout the summer of 1847 vessels crowded with Germans from Hamburg and Bremen were arriving every day at Grosse Isle, "all healthy, robust and cheerful."

So there they were, my father's family: well, not likely on that very ship, but in fact most of them did pack up and leave a little town near Frankfurt-am-Main in that decade. There is a hint of fantasy in the image of those robust and comely young people singing hymns, but seen from the deck of a ship afflicted with typhus and starvation, there must have been a golden haze about those Germans.

What I know about them comes from a small book I inherited from my father, *A History of the Diebel Family, 1736-1936*, which was assembled and published in 1936 by two of my father's aunts, sisters born in the Diebel family who married two Helwig brothers, only one of several connections between the two families. In the eighteenth century the Diebels lived in Niederjossa, Kries Hersfeld, and each child of the large family produced many children. A surprising number of them emigrated to western Ontario and married others of German background. The Helwigs seem to have come from more or less the same area, though they only get noticed when they marry into the Diebel clan.

Genealogy has become a craze by now. As all the world becomes more the same, people want to seek out the particulars of their own history. The Mormons—who face the same problem that led Renaissance intellectuals to puzzle over the fate of "good pagans" and to invent limbo since one hated to think of Virgil in Hell—all have ancestors who lived before the new dispensation, and they have felt compelled to invent a system of baptism for the dead. In order to baptize them retrospectively, you have to find them, so genealogy is crucial.

Societies with a hereditary monarchy, aristocracy or priesthood have always needed to know the pedigree of their citizens, and it may be that the current popularity of genealogy is in part a search for noble or at least notable ancestors. Certainly those envelopes that arrive in the mail offering to trace your family tree and send you a copy of the appropriate crest and motto depend on the assumption that potential customers are longing for something better than a few generations of peasants.

The first international congress on heraldry and genealogy was held in 1928, so the people who assembled the Diebel history in the nineteen-thirties may have been early practitioners in the field. No doubt their own situation, sisters married to brothers who were also second or third cousins, led them to contemplate the importance of family. What is most interesting about the book, 60 years later, is the personal histories, the anecdotes. In some cases, a family member took the trouble to write long narratives while in others nothing is assembled but the facts of birth, marriage and death, names of children. There is a certain bleak poignancy to some of the entries.

Adam Diebel; born in Germany and was married. His wife died leaving him to mourn with an infant. He then emigrated to America with the baby, but it died on the ocean. He came to Buffalo and stayed there for some years. He left Buffalo and has not been heard of since. He was a shoemaker.

Reading that, I hear a verse from the ode to ancestors in Ecclesiasticus: *And some there be that have no memorial, that are perished as if they had never been.*

On the other hand there is a Conrad Diebel—the names recur in the early days, sometimes even two brothers with the same name—who was born in Germany in 1831 and lived 92 years and eight days; nearly a page of close-set type records his life, how he began as a labourer and a shepherd, married and emigrated, his wife seasick for the whole six weeks of the voyage from Bremen.

He stayed with his brother and worked among the farmers during harvest time. In the Fall of 1855 he walked up to Bruce County (a distance of 70 miles) where a cousin had taken up crown land.... He bought 120 acres.... He put up a little shack and a stable. They lived in this shack for nine years and then built a log house which is still used as a dwelling. Their implements consisted of a plough, a harrow made of a limb of a tree, a sickle and a flail. They cleared a few acres every year and tried to seed it with wheat. He carried home flour from Durham, a distance of 18 miles, on his shoulder. Some years, when their wheat looked at its best, the bears would come and trample it down.

My poet daughter is particularly fond of those bears trampling the wheat, a little like something out of a fable, or the brothers Grimm. The man's history is seen by his

45

children, as perhaps he saw it, as a saga of pioneer life, its moral the success that will reward determination and hard work. The description of his personality goes with it.

He was a man of staunch character, decided ideas, and thorough honesty. People came from far and near to seek his counsel.... He died on March 21, 1923, at the age of 92 years and 8 days. They had a family of nine children. He had great influence over his children. His word was law, always having their spiritual welfare in view.

The young labourer and shepherd had become a patriarch. Like most of those described in the book, he was a pillar of the Baptist church. Those who weren't deacons or clerks were likely to sing in the choir, yes, just the kind of people who stood on the deck of that boat at Grosse Ile singing hymns in beautiful harmony, pious and determined.

One of the longest biographies in the book is given to the family's most conspicuous success, Daniel Knechtel. His mother was Anna Eva Diebel, who came to Canada in 1841 and married a man who had emigrated as a child ten years or so earlier. They lived in Waterloo County and Daniel left school at ten, worked as a carpenter and was later apprenticed to a man who made furniture in a small shop attached to his home.

Becoming "of age" and hearing that many new settlers were going into Grey and Bruce counties, Mr. Knechtel decided to strike out for "the Queen's Bush" and in the spring of 1864 he set out to walk to Hanover with a pack of carpenter's tools on his back. It required two days to make the journey. Arriving in Hanover, he found a strong demand for houses and barns and immediately started in the building business. Having built a house for a man named Diebel in Carrick township, he found winter coming on, when outdoor work was impossible, so he moved into the shack which had formerly been the Diebel home, rent free, and began to make furniture, Also, as he was boarding with

46

an older sister (Mrs. John Helwig) who had married, he cut and split cedar rails for his brother-in-law on a basis of 50c per hundred. He used to recall how hard he worked in an effort to average one hundred a day.

That older sister was my great-grandmother. At the time of Daniel Knechtel's marriage, the story goes, he started to make furniture "in a small shack" and in a few years he had created Knechtel Furniture, which by the end of his life employed 400 men in Hanover and had other factories in Walkerton and Southampton. Daniel Knechtel was Hanover's first reeve and an important local philanthropist; a great many of his relatives, close and distant, including my grandfather, one of my uncles, and my father, started work in his factory.

This is the Diebel family's one brush with celebrity. Mostly, at least in the early generations, they worked anonymously as carpenters, cabinetmakers, blacksmiths, shoemakers, or as farmers. Once into the twentieth century, more and more can be seen moving to the cities and engaging in some kind of business. You could count these and calculate and make a chart and call it history, but I prefer the particular flavour of the details, the sense of other times caught in the events and the way they are described; there's the small tragedy of my father's uncle Jacob—I never heard him mentioned, but his fate is there in the book—who died at eight years old when a barn door fell on him. This part of Ontario is only a few miles from Wingham, where Alice Munro grew up, and sometimes one feels an unwritten Munro story behind an entry like this one.

She stayed with her parents and nursed them in their last illness, and after her mother's death she kept house for her father for ten years and after his death in 1923 she went to Kitchener and worked for a furrier for seven years, where she made good. On October 8, 1931, she was married to Andrew Urstadt and they

47

live in Kitchener.

Or this.

She was very particular in performing her domestic duties. In 1895 she went to Preston and worked for George Patterson as maid. They liked her so well that they raised her wages from $6 to $12 per month in two years time. Mrs. Patterson died in 1897 and a new housekeeper was taken in. Lydia left and went to Galt and worked for Hon. George Young.

Mostly the narratives of the men's lives are longer, offering more events in the way of work and travel, but perhaps the longest biography, evidence of the devotion of a son or daughter, is that of an Anna Eva Diebel, born in Ontario in 1847, who married a Baptist minister and ended up in Colorado. Early in her long life, ill health sent her across the border for the first time.

When her brother Jacob had a store in Carlsruhe she kept house for him and worked in the store for about three years. Before this her health was poor and for three months she took treatments in Battle Creek Sanitarium, Battle Creek Michigan, which was then the great Seven Day Advent stronghold and where a strict vegetable diet was given. This brought her down to a skeleton; they also made the Sabbath keeping a vital thing for their patients. They greeted their patients with "Are you a Sabbath keeper?" and strongly impressed them with their religion.

While many of the Diebels emigrated from Germany to Canada and a few to the US, some stayed behind, and the family history recounts the military service of men on both sides of the First World War. Within a page, there are two records of men who lost one finger while serving in the German army. A child was lost to croup while his father was away.

The child died while the father was at war. Word was sent to the father but he did not arrive until the day after the burial. The father insisted on having the corpse lifted to grant him one more look at his darling's face. It was a heart-breaking scene.

48

During this time, my father's oldest brother was with the Canadian infantry. When he was leaving town he gave my father a nickel to go and see *The Beast of Berlin*, which left the boy in tears on behalf of his departed and endangered brother. Later, while my uncle was an observer with the RAF, he was shot down and spent six weeks in a German prison camp before the war ended. Those who wrote the family history make no comment about the family fighting on both sides. In war, you serve the country where you live, no more to be said.

It is the flatness of its narrative that gives this old book its effect. My father annotated his copy, adding the dates of death of his father and each of his brothers: Died March 18, 1950 it says beside the entry for my Uncle Norm. Inside the book are newspaper clippings about the deaths and funerals, including my father's obituary notice, which my mother dutifully added to the collection. I have myself added the dates of death of each of my parents. It seemed right. The book was published two years before I was born, so for me it is complete now.

The later names in the list of 1159 men and woman in the book are Diebels who may or may not have any authentic family connection, like William Frederick Diebel who was born in Hamburg Germany, his ancestors having emigrated from France. The orderly progress of the generations is being dissipated in gossip and false claims. The family history ends with an account, probably reprinted from a local newspaper of a couple—Mr. and Mrs. John Diebel—who were "the longest wed couple in the county of Bruce" having been married for 65 years and raised thirteen children. John Diebel started out in life as a labourer and later began to manufacture pumps. Though the account of this long marriage goes on for some time, it's an epilogue without much pertinence since it's never clear which of the many John Diebels this was, or whether

49

in fact he belongs on the family tree at all. Maybe I could find him if I searched carefully enough, or perhaps he is an honorary addition by reason of name and marital longevity. An achievement is an achievement.

Throughout Western Ontario there were only two couples who could claim to have been married longer than Mr. and Mrs. Diebel.

Their large family was scattered all over north America, as were most of the families in the book even in 1936. By now the grandchildren and great-grandchildren and great-great-grandchildren might be anywhere in the wide world. A family history is like a great river system running in reverse. One begins with the main stream, back in the days of village life when a few pioneers populated a neighbourhood and created a community, but the great river of family runs into an expanding multitude of small channels. There are more and more people in the world each day, always more coupling and giving birth. Perhaps one should picture, not a river running backward into little creeks, but a delta of more and more small channels that eventually become currents within a great sea of all-but-identical molecules.

A Walk Round Hugh MacLennan

Not a guided tour, and there will be no quiz at the end. It may be that the epidemic of education has spoiled us for the desultory, the merely interesting, the occasional, but that's what I have in mind, and I suppose the place to start is the dentist. I think it was a dentist; someone, at any rate, gave my parents a subscription to a magazine, now long vanished, called *The Montrealer*. My first commercial publication was a short story that appeared in that magazine, some years later, so I owe it a double debt since it was in that magazine that I first became acquainted with Hugh MacLennan's work.

The Montrealer was an imitation of *The New Yorker*. It paid less, I suppose, and its circulation was less, and it suffered the indignity of being an obvious imitation, but it served us well in providing a place for Hugh MacLennan to write regular essays. In 1960, he published a collection of 29 essays, and all but three of those had first appeared in *The Montrealer*.

Neither of my parents had a great deal of education. There was a piano in the house, and my mother played it, but while there were a few books, there was none of what you'd call literature, yet something prompted me toward serious books, and those essays of Hugh MacLennan's arrived prompt to the hour. I was reading Hemingway and Steinbeck and working my way through some of Tolstoi and Dostoievsky, but Hugh MacLennan's voice was almost the first Canadian one I remember. It's not easy now, of course, to be sure which essays I read in those lean teenage years, and which I discovered later in books, but there are at least a couple I can be pretty sure of. One of these is "Christmas Without Dickens" and the other is "The Shadow of Captain Bligh." I know I read them early on and neither one is in the 1960 collection.

I remember, in fact, quoting to a friend, older than I was, and a musician, MacLennan's remarks about Haydn and Captain Bligh. He dismissed them, and I suppose that was an early example of something, the clash between the level of a thoughtful observation and the full-dress truth of informed or fashionable opinion. Rereading the essay now, it strikes me that MacLennan was right in his remarks about the freedom of Haydn and the cruelty of Bligh, about the curious moral division of the eighteenth century, or was right enough, and the essay is typical in combining a sharp historical imagination with a resolute refusal to sentimentalize the past. "For all its horrors, the twentieth century is better than the eighteenth; no politician or dictator who has tried to defy its conscience has been able, in the end, to succeed." A nice sentence, and if MacLennan later on in life was less optimistic about where we stand now, he still didn't do one of those sudden about-faces that have been common enough, the socialist who becomes an idolator of capitalism, that kind of thing. MacLennan, the early essays make clear, while he could be playful or whimsical, was above all a serious man, a man who was all of a piece. He was the same man from youth to age, with the same attempt at measured judgment, though the tone of the conclusions changed. Douglas Gibson's selection, *The Best of Hugh MacLennan*, includes a short excerpt from MacLennan's PhD thesis, written for Princeton University, and even there one can find sentences that suggest the manner and sensibility that goes on through all the books. "Civilization," he says at one point, "has always been supported by the patience of the poor, and nowhere were the poor more patient than in Roman Egypt." The balance, clarity, generosity, poise were already present before he was, officially, a writer at all.

There I was, a boy in my teens, wanting to be literate or educated—I'm not sure exactly what it was I wanted, something like that—and there was Hugh MacLennan writing, with a certain easy urbanity, essays about all manner of subjects, essays that still stand up to rereading a lifetime later. His linking of Haydn and Captain Bligh catches perfectly a sense of another world than ours, a different way of being, and it is typical of MacLennan in its double focus, the past and the present. He might almost stand as the perfect example of a certain kind of conservatism, taking the word to mean—what?—perhaps a man who sees every day of his life as rooted in the long human past and judged by it. Marian Engel, who studied with him in the nineteen-fifties said, "I've never worked with anyone, or even talked to anyone who had such a sense of history." He couldn't resist noticing how things came back. Here's how he puts it in one of his essays, that he believes not "that history repeats itself literally but because men and their politics change so little that history often develops similar patterns."

So thanks to the dentist, I was reading Hugh MacLennan at sixteen, and he became some part of an ideal of living and writing. I was reading Hemingway at the same age, of course, and he too was a literary hero, but life has its ways, and my sensibility is probably closer to MacLennan's traditionalist Canadian pattern than to the American modern one that created and destroyed Hemingway—I say this although I love the high modern even if I can't quite claim it as my own.

Then there was *The Watch that Ends the Night*. I was at university in the late fifties, and the great success of MacLennan's book in Canada and the United States was one part of the sudden expansion of Canadian writing. I think it was the same year that Mordecai Richler published *The Apprenticeship of Duddy Kravitz*—MacLennan helped to get him the Canada Council grant that gave him time to write the book—and it was at that time that Irving Layton moved from the little presses to McClelland and Stewart, who brought out *A Red Carpet for the Sun*. Three very different books, but all of them, interestingly, books from Montreal. Richler too was someone I had discovered in *The Montrealer*, which published his short fiction.

The Watch that Ends the Night was the first MacLennan novel I read. It may be his most ambitious book, and was certainly the most successful in both Canada and the United States, and it is a further development of much of the favourite material explored in the earlier novels, the engagement with history, the central figure of an heroic doctor, and, as George Woodcock pointed out many years ago, a story that uses the central plot device of Homer's *Odyssey*. When I first read the book it seemed to me that the love story was the weakest part of it, one reason for this being that MacLennan, in recounting the illness and death of Catherine Stewart, is dealing with the illness and death of his first wife, and he had difficulty finding the distance necessary to turn this into fiction.

The love story is often a problem in MacLennan novels. He liked to attack what he saw as the cynicism and cheapness of treatments of sexual love in twentieth-century fiction. "Since the last war the novel, especially in the United States, has failed worst of all in dealing with the very subject in which it should excel. That subject is love. The fact that the human body was kept out of love by the Victorians seems an inadequate reason for keeping the human soul out of it today. Yet it is a fact that in novel after novel the act of love is treated like the description of a problem in mechanical engineering. My heart sinks when I read through a long narrative dealing with the lives of lawyers or business men and come to the inevitable breaks, like the breaks for a television commercial, in which the hero goes to bed with the wife of his best friend and neither gets any fun out of it." Certainly he's got something there, and the history of sexual narrative in the twentieth century, the mixture of obsession, hysteria and exploitation may still have much to be said about it, but if there is a problem in linking sex and love, it is a problem that MacLennan never solves. His love stories all have moments that are mawkish, and in reading his books, one has to more or less avert one's eyes and get on to other things. It may well be that the link between kindness and lust is humour, and though MacLennan has nice comic moments now and then, he clearly sees nothing funny about the beast with two backs.

Are such attempts to place and define MacLennan's particular strengths and weaknesses, the quality of his work necessary or useful? Why do we do criticism? Gore Vidal, that incorrigible ironist, likes to call it bookchat, legitimately perhaps, for what is it but a conversation about the books we have read. "What is criticism, after all," MacLennan writes in one of his essays, "but the finding of reasons to justify your personal likes and dislikes?"

Well, there are some of us with an inherent desire to put words to things, and one of the subjects we can talk about is what we've read, and by talking or writing about books, we make clear the place they have in our lives, the weight of experience involved in our reading. We want to find our place in history, including literary history. One of the failings of academic criticism is that it must pretend to some kind of grave objectivity. Growing from the roots of scholarship, it often founders in barbarity and pretentiousness in the attempt to have the precision and solidity of a scholarly discipline, when in fact it can be no more than 'bookchat,' a part of an ongoing conversation. Putting things in words as a way to try and understand them.

Still, I cared enough about MacLennan's work to have planned for a long time to write something about it, but the writing always got postponed for one reason or another. Laziness mostly. In fact there may exist somewhere a page or two of an earlier attempt, but the intention was unrealized, and if I'd been asked, Why MacLennan? I'm not perfectly sure I could have answered. At one time I owned copies of pretty well all his books, but when, about to move, I abandoned a couple of thousand books, some of the MacLennan books were among them.

Then, in the summer of 1998, I was in Halifax to attend a wedding, We drove into the city across one of the bridges high over the water, Bedford Basin on the right, the naval base on the left. We were staying downtown, where everything leads uphill to the citadel or downhill to the water. On a beautiful summer afternoon I was at a reception at a private club on the Northwest Arm, and looking across the water of the Arm toward the outer harbour, I saw a huge freighter appear from behind the long peninsula of the downtown and move out of the harbour toward the sea. That image evoked the city's long maritime history. I wanted to read about Halifax, and I had the good luck to find in a second-hand bookstore a cheap 1941 paperback—it cost a quarter originally—of *Barometer Rising*, a MacLennan novel I hadn't read for many years. On the cover the publishers describe it this way: "as exciting a novel as may safely be published." Now there's a tease for you.

Listen to the opening passage of the book.

"He had been walking around Halifax all day, as though by moving through familiar streets he could test whether he belonged here and had at last reached home. In the west the winter sky was brilliant and clouds massing under the sun were taking on colour, but smoke hung low in the streets, the cold air holding it down. He glanced through the dirty window of a cheap restaurant, saw the interior was empty and went in through the double doors. There was a counter, and a man in a soiled apron behind it, a few tables and chairs, and a smell of mustard. He sat on one of the warped stools at the counter and ordered bovril and a ham sandwich."

The tone, the rhythm, the manner, are those of a novelist writing in the tradition of American fiction of the time, someone who has read his Hemingway. Compare this.

"Someone turned on the radio in the wheelhouse. A loud and sentimental song awakened him. He lay there for a moment in his bunk and stared at the square window in the wall opposite him. A sea gull flew lazily by the window. He watched it glide back and forth until it was out of sight."

That's the beginning of another novel published in the same decade, another novel about men and women in wartime, and the general resemblance is clear, though Hemingway is perhaps even more obviously looking over the second writer's shoulder. That second passage is the opening paragraph of *Williwaw*, the first novel by Gore Vidal—before he had become Gore Vidal, we might say. I happened to pick up paperback copies of the two novels at about the same time, and I was struck by some resemblance between the two. Male novels of the nineteen-forties, written in the voice of their time.

I wouldn't want to press the comparison too far. Vidal, who was to develop a very serious engagement with history later on and out of it to produce his best books, doesn't much show it in his first book, but *Barometer Rising* is clearly the work of a man who can't ever forget the presence of the past. Both books have a strong sense of place, but Vidal is writing about an alien place, Alaska, where he did his time in the military, and MacLennan is writing about Halifax, a city where he grew up and for which he had deep personal feelings. I was right to think that rereading the book would give a feeling for the city where I bought the old paperback.

Lying on a bed in the Lord Nelson Hotel, I read the book, which is full of MacLennan's love for a place and a time, Halifax in the days of his boyhood there, the grim December when the collision of two boats produced an explosion that destroyed a great part of the old city. The novel, with its background of shipbuilding, of a war that was fed with men and material by ships sailing out of the Halifax harbour, captures that moment of history in a rich and graceful way. He was writing about a time and place where he was fully at home.

The other novel that grew from MacLennan's early life is *Each Man's Son*. It was his fourth novel, published in 1951. If he had written only these two books, he would still be a significant figure, if a less complex one. Both books are substantial achievements within the conventions of their time, middlebrow books perhaps, but original in looking at the world, previously unknown to fiction, in which he was a boy. It's not an accident that much of the best realistic fiction grows from the life of childhood. For all the documentary power of realism, it is surely a sense of a world informed by something incomprehensible, or only just reaching the fringes of comprehension, that gives realistic fiction its power.

The central character in *Each Man's Son* is a version of MacLennan's own father. One could read many things into the fact that in the novel this father is childless and at-tempts to commandeer another man's son, that the child's true father is a physically powerful, inarticulate, brutal man, but whatever one makes of this imaginary geneal-ogy, the detail of the novel is solid. Though MacLennan's family made some effort to shield themselves from the

58

harsher sides of Cape Breton life, his depiction of a punch-drunk fighter is very well done, and the miners and their wives are portrayed with love and humour. MacLennan's mixture of history and myth in the portrayal of these lost Highlanders is convincing, and the simple story moves toward an ending that is as right and as arbitrary as tragedy. It has its uncomfortable moments when MacLennan writes about sexual love, but as a whole, it has about it the kind of truth that fiction can achieve.

That at least is my reading of the book. It wasn't one of MacLennan's favourites; he thought it was "muddy," and he said of it, "I must say it was written during one of the times of my life when I was unhappy." It was, in terms of sales, his least successful up to that time, and in order to make a living, he wrote a great many articles and essays for magazines, as well as beginning to teach part time at McGill. For a while, he was writing something like 30 articles a year. This is the period when he wrote the essays that I came upon in *The Montrealer*, and for all the speed with which he was working, he doesn't give the impression of a man who was writing more than he had to say.

I'd got this far in thinking about MacLennan when I discovered that there was a Hugh MacLennan novel I had never read, and one that was, for at least a time in the nineteen-fifties, his favourite. I used to own a paperback copy of *The Precipice*, and I assumed that I must have read it, though I couldn't remember it clearly, but when I found a library copy and began, I discovered that it was all new to me. *The Precipice* is MacLennan's American novel. It is about an American engineer who comes to a small town in Eastern Ontario, and about the woman from that town who becomes his wife, and a good deal of the novel takes place in the United States. Let me tell you some of the things I thought while I was reading it. The context of the novel is the years after the second war, the years when I was growing up, and it belongs with the novels of that time. Reading a scene about upper-middle-class life in New York City, I thought that this was the kind of thing I read in my teens that gave me a picture of what adult life might be, though on the whole my adult life was never much like that. This was a time when naughty books were things like *Forever Amber* and *Tobacco Road*, perhaps *Gone with the Wind*. Even MacLennan was accused by Canadian reviewers of being too sexy. It was a period when MacLennan could observe that in fictional construction, "a good woman is an enemy to a good plot." Since then, of course, women have stopped being good. Plots too perhaps. It was around this time that MacLennan dismissed as "decadent" a list of novelists including Proust, Joyce, Thomas Mann, Aldous Huxley and Evelyn Waugh. What this all amounts to is that he was immersed, and happily enough, in the world of the middlebrow in its period of triumph, though by placing his two Nova Scotia novels in the past, he gave them a window on another world.

All that said, let me go on to remark that *The Precipice* is not a bad book. It is very concentrated, treating only four or five characters, and though it's not a short book, it has the precise focus of a miniature. The study of the frustration of a well-meaning but uninspired man trying to succeed is interesting, if much of its time. The writing is workmanlike, but the story moves along.

It was while reading *The Precipice* that I remembered a letter I got from a friend a few years ago. It was 1985, and the three-hundredth anniversary of the birth of J.S. Bach was being celebrated, by the CBC at least. The radio was full of concerts and documentaries about his life, and this friend said he'd just been reminded that Bach was a schoolmaster, and he thought that said a lot about him. For some reason it popped back into my mind as I was reading *The Precipice*. MacLennan was a schoolmaster for a while, though he got out when he could, and his particular level of seriousness and propriety does have a slight odour of chalkdust. The love of generalizing and an optimism that can seem almost programmatic are part of this.

It was just after I'd been reading *The Precipice* that I discovered the published collection of letters exchanged by MacLennan and Marian Engel. I didn't know MacLennan, but I did know Marian Engel, at least professionally, and I liked her and her work. The exchange of letters is full of empty spaces—MacLennan answering letters of Marian's that have vanished, so that in the early period, the only voice we hear is MacLennan's, but there are quotations from her MA thesis, which he supervised, and one can sense her presence there in the spaces, and at the end of the book there is a short account of their friendship that she wrote for a conference much later on. What was most interesting about the book is that a slight sense of claustrophobia I'd felt, reading one MacLennan novel after another, vanished in reading his letters. I've always suspected we read MacLennan's novels in order to read beyond them to the mind and spirit lying behind, and in the letters, when he is writing in his own voice, his generosity of spirit, his unpedantic seriousness, are the things closest at hand.

Time to turn to the matter of Quebec. It was in 1945 that MacLennan published his second novel, *Two Solitudes*, the one that established him as a public writer, as someone who was determined to confront the problems of Canadian political and social life, the relationship of French and English in this country. The first printing of the book sold out on the day of publication.

Not long ago, I was looking for something in microfilm of old issues of *Le Devoir*, copies from the middle seventies, and there I found, by complete accident, an article (highly favourable, just imagine) on Mordecai Richler, that mentions in passing MacLennan's book—*cette ennuyeuse brique d'un livre*, the journalist called it. The novel can be seen, I suppose, as a view from Westmount—though it tries not to be—and certainly no-one who writes for *Le Devoir* is likely to have much sympathy for the view from Westmount.

There is always a possible problem when a writer tries to get inside an alien culture, the problem that has recently been expressed—in a militant and not always subtle way—in debates about the appropriation of voice. The tendency of that debate, of course, is to suggest that we can only write about what is close to us, even, finally, only write about ourselves, and in this way politics buttresses a regrettable tendency to solipsism that is already present in the culture. You whine about your sorrow and I'll whine about mine.

When MacLennan talked later on about his decision to write about the life of French Canada, he quoted the old saw, "Fools rush in where angels fear to tread." His biographer suggests that his treatment is heavily indebted to Ringuet's *Trente Arpents*. However that may be, the most convincing characters in the book are the French ones, and in fact the best of all is a character that MacLennan disapproves of, the angry nationalist Marius Tallard, son of the old *seigneur* Athanase Tallard, central character of the first part of the book, and half-brother of Paul Tallard, the hero of the book's last section. Perhaps this only goes to show that the devil still has all the best tunes.

I say that—the best character, the most convincing— but what does it mean? The question of how we judge characters in fiction is one that has puzzled me since I was a high-school student. The judgment of what is credible depends on our own experience of literature and life, and so does the judgment of what is interesting. Literary style can be quoted, examples set side by side, but a fictional character is a construction, in words and then in the imagination. If I say that Marius Tallard is a powerful, convincing and sufficiently complex character, and you say no, is there any basis for discussion?

Still, I am prepared to say that the scenes with Marius in them come to life in the imagination; they have the vitality of the best fiction. So do other things in the book. The confrontation between the aristocratic Athanase Tallard and the parish priest, Father Beaubien, two stubborn men locked in battle, has what fiction can offer. There is a fine scene in which Captain Yardley, an old Nova Scotia sea-captain, is telling a ribald story about a mare and a stallion while his repressed and narrow daughter is trying to deal with the news of her husband's death. And the death of Athanase Tallard is finely done.

The writing about the relationships of men and women is, for much of the book, without the sad falling away that sometimes happens in MacLennan, partly because he is not trying to describe romantic love, only to show, as the best realists showed, how this complicated thing plays itself out. Toward the end, the book grows weaker as it falls away from tragedy to romance, and we find a passage like this one.

"Suddenly talk seemed stupid. He turned and took her in his arms and his lips found hers. Desire broke within him like an explosion. He felt the firmness of her back against the palms of his hands, her breasts yielding against his chest, her hips...." Well, that's enough. Here we can say exactly what the trouble is. MacLennan, for whatever reason, has yielded entirely to cliché, to the worst and emptiest kind of language. The question of why this happens may be an interesting one, but the passage itself has nothing to say.

Turn from that to a short passage at the beginning of the account of the death of Athanase Tallard, a man who

63

was a mixture of dignity and folly, who has ended up bankrupt and lost.

"Athanase breathed; he existed, he lay in the sheets and heard as though from a great distance the mechanism which held the life in him running down. It was morning; the sunlight streamed in the window and sparkled on the snow-covered roof next door. It was afternoon, and the snow was purple with shadows. A shaded lamp showed it was night. But for him no real time had passed because he could not measure it. His mind was like water coloured by changing weather."

That last brilliant simile. The whole passage of several pages is wonderfully done, with the sense of inevitability and complication in the responses of those who watch the death, his second wife, a kind, shallow, sensual woman, his son Marius, desperate that his father should return to the church on his deathbed.

It takes no great critical insight to suggest that the book loses some of its energy after the death of Tallard, but MacLennan wanted to look into the years following his death, to see where history went, and the loss of energy is an example of one of the difficult things about the novel, that a perfectly good idea may refuse to embody itself.

An interesting side issue raised by *Two Solitudes*. Much of the dialogue in the book is a rendering, in English, of dialogue that we know took place in French. This is a convention, and often we accept it without question. When Athanase and the priest argue, they speak literate English which we know is to be taken as the equivalent of literate French. But with the characters who are less literate there may be more of a problem, as also with the "bad French" of Captain Yardley. This intrigues me since it's a problem that I have dealt with at first hand. A few years ago, I translated the last six stories of Anton Chekhov.

One of the reasons I decided to do it was that after doing one of them as an exercise, I looked at a well-reputed translation, and discovered that the translator had rendered Russian colloquial speech as some kind of stereotyped cockney. Stupid, and I was convinced that I could do better than that. Still, the problem of rendering dialogue that sounds natural in English while it doesn't drag the whole story into the wrong culture or the wrong century is a difficult one. It's a little like the complex technical problem of writing a sonnet or *terza rima*, and MacLennan's attempts at it are sometimes a little offhand. But on the whole *Two Solitudes*—the smart young journalist in *Le Devoir* to the contrary—is a brave and powerful book. Perhaps predictably, when it was published the reviewer in *La Presse* loved it, the reviewer in *Le Devoir* hated it. One of the most interesting comments was in a review by Diana Trilling in the American periodical *The Nation*. What she says, it seems to me, applies not just to this novel but to much of MacLennan's work. "Mr. MacLennan's novel," she wrote, "is more workmanlike than gifted. I suspect, then, that we have in this case one of those rare instances in which an author's seriousness and decency do a very good job as proxy for art."

It was twenty years later that MacLennan returned to the matter of Quebec, the political problems of our odd situation as a place that is perhaps two countries or perhaps no country at all.

It was in 1967, the year of the Canadian centennial celebrations, that he published his sixth novel, *The Return of the Sphinx*. Read now, it is a troubled and troubling book, and it's hard to know where to begin in thinking about it. As a work of art, there is much to be said against it, and perhaps not a lot to be said in its defence. It is a book about Canada and Quebec, and MacLennan cared passionately about both, but he was unable to find a story to embody his concerns. The book alternates largely un-convincing fiction with impassioned lectures, and it contrives to be both grim and naïve, but the reasons for this are worth consideration.

MacLennan was deeply disturbed by the tendency toward violence in the Quebec nationalism of his time, and *The Return of the Sphinx* can in some ways be regarded as a prophetic book. It was published, remember, three years *before* the War Measures Act crisis, the double kidnapping and the murder of Pierre Laporte. The book was written during the period when FLQ bombings were taking place in Montreal, and MacLennan set out to tell a story set in this context, though he meant it to apply to a worldwide phenomenon. And in many ways it does: I was reminded recently of the murder of Aldo Moro by the Red Brigades, which also occurred a few years later.

Still, for all we praise the power of imagination, as I said earlier, any writer has great limitations in writing about an alien society, and the French society of Quebec, especially in a situation of sudden and swift change, as it was in the sixties, was deeply alien to MacLennan, even though he had lived for years in Montreal.

MacLennan was no fool, and he recognized the problem, (though in *Two Solitudes* he just went right ahead and wrote about *québécois* from the inside—but that was in 1945, in a more innocent world) and his solution is to make his young revolutionary half-Anglo, the son of a character revived from *Each Man's Son*. This, of course, is a solution that only exacerbates the problem, making it perfectly obvious that his character represents no-one, or to put it more precisely, he represents certain attitudes of MacLennan's, but he has no convincing fictional existence. The attempt to make him stand for what MacLennan sees as an almost childish rebelliousness in the young, the sixties generation, and to make this stand for the violent

66

anger of groups like the FLQ, is one of the things that makes the novel seem naïve.

Yet side by side with this, some of the book's potted lectures suggest that MacLennan was not without sophistication in his understanding of the forces in play. That he was frightened by them isn't surprising, though it's possible to argue that he took too seriously what was a merely peripheral contemporary phenomenon, a criminal corollary to the real historical truths. He was, later on, one of those who idealized Pierre Trudeau—one more example, one might suggest, of an enduring tendency to hero-worship—and he saw the invoking of the War Measures Act as a dangerous but necessary move, emergency surgery of the sort that the doctors in his novels are apt to perform.

Return of the Sphinx is the novel of a frightened and angry man, frightened not just of the situation in Quebec, but of the world that appeared to be undergoing violent changes everywhere, with a lot of loose talk of revolution, and much talk, and a certain amount of action, about sexual freedom. It was, after all, MacLennan's hero Pierre Trudeau who set out, sensibly, perhaps even nobly, to get the state out of the bedrooms of the nation. I am not yet a senior citizen, but I can remember the days when any homosexual behaviour was against the law. In fact I have worked with a man who—this happened in England—was sent to prison for being a homosexual.

MacLennan started out as a student of the falling Roman Empire, and licentiousness would always be, for him, an aspect of decadence. It's possible he was right, but it's also possible that he simply took human sexuality too seriously. Look back to another decent, public-spirited novelist, Henry Fielding, and you see a man who regarded human desire as an expression of high spirits and an essentially comic matter.

It all reminds me of events in the United States, where a great many members of the Republican Party, seeing the sixties as a kind of original sin still awaiting retribution, regarded Bill Clinton's adventures as the embodiment of corruption, while most of the country was content to make more and more ingenious cigar jokes. And while I'm looking south, let me give another glance toward Gore Vidal, who seems to be following this essay like an elegant ghost. He, like MacLennan, was fascinated by history, but one reason for his greater success in dealing with parts of it is that he loved politics and politicians with all their failings and corruptions, while MacLennan disliked and distrusted most of them.

Return of the Sphinx is a very odd book. It's odd, for example, that MacLennan, a man who never had children, sees the conflict of generations as an Oedipal battle between fathers and sons, that as a teacher who wrote of being happy among the young, his attitude to the young people of this book seems mostly to be resentment. The only young person who is approved of falls in love with a man her father's age, in fact a friend of her father. The book has all of the grim pessimism of Freud, but none of his careful pragmatic feeling for human betterment. "I flatter myself," he said in a letter to Marian Engel about the writing of the book, "that I was able to break through empathetically into this new world of the nineteen-sixties." He was wrong.

The book perhaps is something more like a symptom than a work of art. MacLennan may well have been right in his sense that the past is dying. If there is no longer anything that deserves reverence, there will soon enough be nothing that deserves respect. The end of deference, as it has been called, may have been allied to the liberation of blacks, gays, women, but those—MacLennan certainly, but I would include myself as well—who have an attachment to continuity, to the ongoing of something unchangeable, may sometimes feel themselves at sea in a storm, the light failing. That's not a bad image, derived from one of its best passages, for *The Return of the Sphinx*.

Elspeth Cameron's biography of MacLennan quotes from a number of the extremely negative reviews of the book, especially from the smart-alec young reviewers of Toronto. Young reviewers like Robert Fulford and Peter Gzowski. How quickly time passes. The book came out in 1967, the year of Expo, when we were all being very clever and declaring the newness of the new world here in Canada. This was the year, Cameron points out, when Leonard Cohen published *Beautiful Losers*, another book about history and Montreal. For all his idealizing of Pierre Trudeau, MacLennan represented, to the clever, the same kind of things they saw and mocked in Robert Stanfield, decency, dignity and a lack of flash. There was a kind of adolescent energy abroad then, and we were all very sophisticated.

At more or less the same time he was writing a book that signally failed to catch the texture and meaning of the present moment, MacLennan was writing the two versions of *Rivers of Canada*. It's interesting that his second wife told his biographer that "the real Hugh" was found in that book. Here he was engaged with the adventurous history and striking geography of the country he loved, and his unease with many elements of the contemporary world is left behind.

Canada, the world, and war, were the subjects of Hugh MacLennan's first novel, and the subject of his last. In some ways, it is a return to the problems that concerned him in *Return of the Sphinx*, but the book is much more successful.

Voices in Time, published in 1980, is set in the future, a future closer now than twenty years ago when the book appeared. I'm not a reader of science-fiction or futuristic novels. Neither, I expect, was Hugh MacLennan, and it's easy enough to look at his assumptions about the future and find places where he is wrong, but any novel set in the future is in some ways simply a metaphorical way of talking about the present and the past, and some, at least, of the book's themes are as apt now as they ever were. The most telling is the presentation of the corrupting effect that entertainment has on journalism. Perhaps he didn't need to be especially prescient to understand this, but it's a central element in *Voices in Time.*

The events take place in an era when a catastrophic and probably accidental war has wiped out most life on the planet. The past has been lost, even the memory of that great catastrophe. The ruling powers have tried to wipe out all knowledge of the past, but one of MacLennan's insights is that even those who have lost the knowledge of history are immersed in a progress that is historical. This is the book of MacLennan's old age, and its grim power comes from a sense of our immersion in cycles of history. The Roman empire, the Nazi empire, some new empire that is perhaps without a name—the recurrence of some terrible inevitability.

The book is, of course, as pretty much always in MacLennan, about fathers and sons, and the love stories have some of the usual weaknesses. MacLennan takes on the impossible in trying to write, at least tangentially, about the Holocaust, and it seems to me makes a greater error in using it as an element in his plot. One section of the book suggests a boy's adventure story when what he is trying to talk about is human weakness in the face of evil.

The more interesting questions have to do with the view of history and the present, the question of whether his sense of terrible decline is the expression of what all aging men are apt to feel because the world is changing or whether MacLennan has caught something real. This is especially true with regard to the FLQ acts of violence and the kidnappings of 1970. Looking back, it's not easy to decide whether that was a large and significant event or a grotesque small one. The War Measures Act was passed because of "an apprehended insurrection," and there's some question about whose feeling of apprehension was being calmed. And certainly we had a generation or more of political violence in the world around that time.

MacLennan treats the events in Quebec as an example of a disorder that was occurring throughout the world, the result, in part, of allowing rebels to dramatize themselves in public, what might be called, though it's my phrase, not his, a kind of political sentimentality. And yet, though he is fearful of rebellion, he sees all civilizations, going back to the Roman one which was his first object of study, as beset and constricted by centralizing bureaucracies that gradually weigh down the activities of the citizens with rules and taxes.

So he's on both sides, or neither, and for a novelist that's fair enough. The greatness of Tolstoi's novels is informed by his spiritual struggles, and the novels would have been less if the struggles had been resolved. MacLennan is not by any means Tolstoi, but in his struggle to understand History and Spirit, he is in the same—is it Hegelian?—tradition. For all *Voices in Time* predicts a dark future, its conclusion is optimistic. After the great disaster, a few committed and intelligent young people set out to relearn history and to rebuild the world.

If you want unflawed artistic perfection, you don't read MacLennan, but for all its flaws, *Voices in Time* has some kind of metaphorical resonance, at least to me reading it now. Nearly twenty years after its publication, the following passage, set in the future, looking back at where we are now, is telling.

"Furious voices spewed out hatred and loathing against my whole generation. *We* were the spoiled brats who had been responsible for all their woes. *We* were the ones who had destroyed their authority over their children and foisted our own laziness and sensuality onto everyone else. *We* were the ones who had insisted on abolishing capital punishment, had sneered at the police, had sympathized with the murderer and not with his victim, had pretended that crime is the fault of society as a whole and not of the criminal."

Could there be a better summary of the resentful attitudes that have caused liberal to be a bad word in many circles? Bring back Captain Bligh, and perhaps we'll get Haydn with him. The passage, presumably, is not there to present MacLennan's own position, but he has heard and felt what is in the air, and something in the old man can hear an echo of at least some part of truth in the sound. He was a Calvinist trained as a classical historian, and a life without discipline is not one he would ever have understood.

I deliberately waited until I'd been through all the other MacLennan novels to return to *The Watch that Ends The Night* and read through it again, for the first time in several years. I decided that the Encyclopedia of Familiar Assumptions is right in thinking it his best. It is a very impressive book, and I see now many ways in which reading and rereading it when I was young helped to create my view of the history of this century. Going back, I found that I saw it, particularly the ending, in a different way than I did when I was twenty or thirty. The long passages about life and death, about the way the individual exists in and out of chaos, walk terribly close to portentousness and sentimentality at times, and when I was younger, I felt they tumbled into the abyss, or at least dropped one foot onto the slippery slope, but now I find the ending moving and haunting, partly for the way it faces hatred and anger and yearns toward meaning and comfort. Its struggle with ultimate questions has its own integrity, and we know it is informed by the pain of the long illness and premature death of MacLennan's first wife. One of Elspeth Cameron's more astute critical comments in her biography concerns the overlap between the voice heard in the essays of the fifties and the first-person narrative of the novel. George Stewart is not MacLennan and yet there is some ghostly link. That double exposure, which a certain kind of critic would call a failing, isn't— the opposite in fact. We hear echoes in the space between two levels of reality, and the music of these echoes lasts. As I read the last section of the novel, I thought that some measure of the book's precarious balance, its tender achievement of a large serenity, can be registered in the fact that in MacLennan's next book, *Return of the Sphinx*, all of it was lost. Critics speak of art as if its achievements were easily accounted for by some kind of critical formula, but in fact the hard work goes on and on and only sometimes does lightning strike. Art is not mystification, but its accomplishments are mysterious. A sense of struggle and confusion is part of what gives the book its power.

To look over the career of one of the men who created whatever literary culture we possess is an act of respect, and a useful antidote to the urgency of the wired world. One sees writing as a struggle to create something solid out of a specific personality in a specific time. That's how we all start and what we all hope to achieve. Something at least momentarily transcendent. Academic critics like to lecture writers, to tell them what they should have done, but they are armchair generals who weren't there when the battle was going on. One of the most astute critical remarks I've ever read was by V.S. Pritchett who wrote somewhere that a writer's strengths are usually the same as his weaknesses.

The imagination makes what it can of our experience, struggles toward the transcendence that is art, when what we write is more than what we are. And most terrible: that what we are, though it's all we have, is no excuse.

Monsieur Valentin

Toronto, one afternoon, in winter I think, and with time on my hands I wander into the Art Gallery of Ontario. As a freelance writer living in Kingston, I was back and forth to Toronto a good deal, often just for the day, and I had a personal list of available public washrooms, useful when you're walking the streets, and the AGO, clean, warm, accessible, was at the top of the list. There were days when I only used the toilets and had a look around the gallery shop, but on other occasions I paid my admission and spent time in the galleries.

It was in one of the large rooms running parallel to the front wall of the building that I stopped by an unfamiliar painting. It was a large work, perhaps six feet high by nine long, and a little dim, with the dramatic action of the painting appearing out of the umber shadows in the way of much seventeenth-century work. It was fascinating, yet somehow unfamiliar, and I looked at it for a long time, all those faces with a slightly greenish cast to the skin, and then I went over to read the label and find out who'd painted it: Valentin de Boulogne.

A new name to me, and now years later, I know only a little more about him than I did that day. He was a Frenchman, apparently born in 1594, though other sources give earlier dates, and he spent much of his working life in Rome and died there in 1632, one of the genre painters influenced by Caravaggio. It is said that he lived a bohemian life and his death reflected it. Not much has been written about him; I have only ever seen one monograph, written in Italian and on sale in the bookstore of the Louvre for a price high enough that I didn't feel able to buy it. At that point, I thought I might use the paintings of Valentin in a novel, but the novel changed.

There were thirteen figures in the painting I discovered on that winter afternoon in Toronto. Thirteen characters and a number of intersecting stories appear in fragments out of the darkness. The scene, presumably, is the public room of an inn. At the rear a flat wall, and at the viewer's left, a group of musicians, an old man with grey hair and a beard playing a large viol in the foreground, in the background, two other men, one plucking a lute or theorbo, the other bowing a stringed instrument, and between, a young woman at a small portable organ and a boy singing. The young man with the lute and the girl at the keyboard look straight out at the viewer, the only characters in the painting who do.

At the other end of the long horizontal painting is a scene of incipient violence. A man in armour, a soldier presumably, appears to be intervening between two men, one with his fist raised to strike. This is in the top corner and is seen in bits of highlight among the shadows. In the brightest passage of the work, a fortune-teller with a dark complexion, a moor or gypsy, touches the extended hand of a young man whose red shirt flashes through the openings in his metal armour. The fortune-teller wears a white scarf over her head and shoulders, and a blue tunic with a red sash. The other figures in the painting are isolated observers; a woman in the foreground appears to be looking at something outside the frame.

My description of the painting comes not from the memory of that initial discovery but from a colour photocopy made out of a slide I bought later on. The painting is not owned by the AGO but is on long-term loan from the anonymous owners, and to buy the slide I had to send a letter promising that it would be used only for purposes of research. I had the photocopy made since it was larger and easier to consult, and at some time afterward, during a move, I misplaced the slide itself. So what I have available to give an account of the painting is a long way from the original, the colours coarse and inadequate, but it shows the painting's structure, the way it tells its stories.

As I said, one of the striking characteristics of the original is the tint of the skin. The round-faced, attractive young woman who stares out of the painting with an odd, uninterpretable look has a curious pallid colour achieved by a scumbling of greenish blue paint or glaze over the original, more apparently natural colours. The painting of the other faces is similar. This gives the whole painting its own strange mood, and it was this more than anything that caught my attention as I walked by for the first time. It was an intense and mysterious drama appearing out of darkness, the visual organization powerful, the painting of the faces skilled and subtle.

There is only one painting by Valentin documented to a certainty, a scene of martyrdom in the Vatican, but there are paintings attributed to him scattered about the world. There are two Biblical paintings in the Musée des Beaux Arts in Montreal, one of Abraham and Isaac, a striking small painting with a vulnerable, crouching boy about to be sacrificed, the familiar odd tint to the skin, and across the room, a version of King David that is both brighter than usual at the centre and darker at the circumference.

Then there is the Louvre. Cardinal Mazarin collected the works of Valentin, and his collection is now divided between Versailles and the Louvre. I took a camera with me the second time I went, to record the paintings I saw. I have some of the photographs in front of me. There are four genre paintings in one of the galleries of seventeenth-century French art, and on the opposite wall, a couple of Biblical scenes. The genre paintings are smaller than the one in Toronto, but what is most striking about them is that they are closely parallel to it and to each other, to the point of using nearly all the same models, the Valentin de

Boulogne repertory company. It's not unknown for artists to use the same model more than once—Rembrandt's wives, Manet's family and friends—or the same clothing—Vermeer's yellow fur-trimmed jacket—but I'm not aware of anyone else who repeatedly painted the same group of people in more or less the same costumes and in what is apparently the same location.

The dark-skinned fortune-teller appears in two of the Louvre paintings. In one she holds a glass of wine in her hand and is picking the pocket of a young musician who is playing a recorder, and in the other she is having her pocket picked by a man with a black bandanna around his head who is almost hidden in the shadow at the edge of the picture. In both cases she wears the blue tunic over a white shirt or shift. What appears in the Toronto picture to be a red sash, looks like a red stripe on the edge of the tunic in one of the Louvre paintings, but she is vividly the same figure, a heavy body, upright, unbending, still of course, but with an implicit sense of slow and dignified movement, heavy red beads around her throat lying against the brown skin, immense presence to her, as of some great lady of the stage.

The round-faced girl is in at least two of the Louvre pictures, perhaps three or four. It's not quite clear whether the woman musician in the other two pictures is the same woman, or only a similar one. In one of the scenes, the girl sits behind a table with some sort of meat-filled pastry on it, plays a guitar and again looks toward the viewer with a look that is hard to describe—timid, knowing too much, a sensuous mouth and wise eyes. None of that is more than my impression, perhaps, but in three of the five paintings I'm describing here, a female musician looks out of the picture and meets the eyes of the painter, our eyes. Feminist critics have written about the women in paintings as on display, offering a naked body, a gaze that encourages you to look back, to take possession. In one of Valentin's inn scenes, the girl wears a low-cut dress that reveals the tops of her breasts, which are compressed upward to be visible, and in that painting, she leans on the shoulder of a man in a plumed hat who is pouring wine, and she watches the fortune-teller's face while the dark woman picks a pocket. The face that watches, the lips slightly parted, the eyes wide, alert, is both immensely vulnerable and immensely sexual. If she is meant to be a whore—a standard interpretation of such genre scenes—she is one who has not lost her moral innocence.

Imaginative speculation: seventeenth-century paintings with their theatrical sense of a scene interrupted at a crucial moment encourage it. In this set of paintings by Valentin, because the same faces recur, we are faced with a double puzzle, the meaning of the pose and expression within a single painting, and the sense of the same faces reappearing in slightly different situations but with certain similar qualities in each case. The bearded old man appears in two of the secular paintings, once playing a viola da gamba, once playing a small harp and singing. His concentration, in each case, is on himself and his music. In one of the Biblical paintings, which both represent dramatic moments of judgment—Solomon and Daniel—the old man is one of the lecherous elders accusing the innocent Susanna. The model for Susanna, is—I want to say of course—the same as for the perplexing and intriguing girl musician. The bearded old man may also have given his face to Abraham in the painting in Montreal, but I have no copy of it in front of me, and my memory of it is not sufficiently vivid for me to be certain. How much of what I see in any of these paintings will still be present if I set the photographs aside? Do I truly remember if I only know in words what I once saw?

Of the other male figures in these scenes in a seven-

79

teenth-century inn—sinister swarthy types, one art historian calls them—the most striking is a man with a straight sharp nose and a moustache. He has a detached air. To play as cast: he has a number of roles, a cynical drinker and watcher, but also the man who waits to have his future told by the gypsy. He wears varying costumes, but never the red shirt and bronze armour. That goes to someone else. The young boys are a raffish lot, singing enthusiastically with wide-open mouths, drinking down wine from a jug in the dim background, or staring out of the scene, head leaning on a hand, elbow on the table, looking about while someone else turns the pages of the small book of music.

Technically the paintings are closely similar, the chiaroscuro, the horizontal organization of the figures, the painting of the flesh dimmed by the strange green that is thinly laid over the warmer tones, making every scene a little haunted. Who was this Valentin, with his familiar manner and his little theatre troupe playing out scenes of life? Once, in a magazine on art and the art market, I found a photograph of a painting attributed to Valentin that had recently sold and was without the familiar qualities. No doubt there were good reasons for the attribution, but at first glance the eye rejected it. Several of the paintings shown in books or catalogues are closer to the manner of Caravaggio, or to Manfredi, who was, they say, more than Caravaggio himself, the inventor of the low-life scene as a subject. Of course Valentin was a minor figure, and there will be no group of scholars like those of the Rembrandt project setting out to decide which paintings are by the master. Perhaps the Rembrandt project's rejection (for a few years at least; they seem to have changed their minds now) of a great painting like the Polish Rider in the Frick will make us all more aware of what all the experts surely know, that there were wonderful artists beyond the famous names.

If I were a scholar, I would go to the museums and begin to learn more about the provenance of the paintings by Valentin in their collections, or I would go to Rome and look for documentation of his life. No doubt the author of the Italian monograph has already done this, but where I live the book is not available, and it may be that I prefer not to know too much. The biography of long-vanished artists is always an uncertain business. The death of Valentin sounds like a legend. Overheated by wine and tobacco, he was staggering through the streets of Rome, plunged into the Fontana de Babuino, took cold and died. That may be true, or may not. The inner life of his paintings, the interplay, has its own necessity—those writing about him use words like brooding and melancholy—reinforced by his comparative anonymity. In a book on Caravaggio one finds a copy of a lost painting by the master, the copy attributed to the Circle of Valentin. We have little enough information about Valentin; what are we to make of his circle? Still, I don't mind this drift into uncertainty and speculation. Some day in a strange place, Cologne or Toulouse or Poughkeepsie, I may find another arrangement of the familiar faces.

On that first winter afternoon in Toronto, I wrote a few words in a small notebook and went back out to Dundas Street, and later I got on the train. A few years later, at the Musée des Beaux Arts in Montreal, I walked away from the paintings and stood to watch the thickly falling snow through one of those long narrow windows that look up avenue du Musée, the steep street that rises toward the bare trees on the mountain. Later still, in the Louvre, I looked out a window, and a line of walkers was crossing the paving stones of the Cour Napoléon in a light September rain, one wearing red slacks and carrying a red umbrella, going out of sight.

Time Present

You go looking for one thing and you find another. I had taken myself off to the Canadian Centre for Architecture in downtown Montreal to see an exhibition of photographs by Edouard Baldus, pictures of buildings in France taken in the years after 1852, and the large-scale photographs, brown and pale gold, left me thinking about time and photography, about the ways we apprehend the past. The factualness of photography, its grip on actuality.

All the time, down the hall, or through an archway, I could see bits of another exhibition, and later I made my way along the hall to see what was there. It was a selection of work by a Canadian architect of Jamaican background, Richard Henriquez. What was on show was not his buildings, though there were photographs of some of them. It was an exhibition of drawings, models, sculptures, and something called The Memory Theatre.

The Memory Theatre is a circle of wooden cabinets, with an opening at one side so that you can walk into the circle. At the centre is a freestanding sculpture, a globe, on a tripod. The cabinets, mostly vertical with a small horizontal unit about waist level, are constructed of wood, with glass doors. Inside, on shelves, a wide variety of objects are displayed, architectural maquettes, small sculptures, found objects, toys. All of these things have personal connections with the architect and his family. The horizontal units contain family documents and photographs.

The notes to the exhibition talk about various sources and parallels for the memory theatre, going back to "memory theatres" used as an orator's notebook in the Renaissance, to the tradition of the cabinet of curiosities

82

in a rich man's house, also to certain constructions by Marcel Duchamp. The notes don't mention another parallel that sprang to my mind, the boxes made by the American artist Joseph Cornell. In every case objects are given concentrated attention because of their place in a box and beside other strange objects. The simplest things can become far-fetched.

Richard Henriquez's Memory Theatre is an appealing work, and while I saw it on show in a museum, that's not what it was made for. After the exhibition, it was to go back to the room in his house for which it was designed. I spent some time looking at those curiosities in their wooden cabinets, admiring them, and then I walked away with some odd feelings about art and time.

One of the functions of the aesthetic is to conquer time. Richard Henriquez has made his past into a piece of design, and splendidly so. The installation exists in some middle ground where art meets decoration, architecture meets memory. The Baldus photographs that I'd been examining in another part of the gallery were images of how things looked over a hundred years ago; time, as we say, stood still. One part of the impulse to make art is the impulse to perfection, to achieve something finished and silent. The haunting stillness is a part of its power, but that stillness is also a kind of death.

A personal example: I own an old house that I renovated over the course of a few years, doing most of the work myself, and, since it's a summer place with no heat or running water, I was guided mostly by how things look. It's full of strange things; it's my own memory theatre if you like. One day I was sitting in one of the rooms, one that was finished and that satisfied me, and I looked around and thought to myself, Yes, this is fine, this is beautiful. I should burn it down.

At that moment what I saw around me felt complete,

and anything complete is a kind of prison.

Now in the case of an old house, wind and snow and rain and birds and mice will prevent an excessive perfection, and yet I think the conflict I felt at that moment was a real one. If we strive to shape our environment to a certain aesthetic ideal, the ideal shaping is closed and final, like those wooden cabinets in Henriquez's Memory Theatre or the photographs from another century, moments isolated from the flow of time. All such stillness is an illusion, perhaps. Time and death conquer most things, but for a while what we have put together seems to be at rest, and we have to seek out new spaces to shape, the future perfect.

2

My father was a craftsman who worked with his hands. He took old pieces of furniture that were worn and damaged and restored them to beauty and use. There is a kind of poetry about old things, but an affection for what has been can become merely antiquarian and reactionary, a flight from the present, from where we are. I've enjoyed the traces of the past in the landscape where I've lived, the old limestone houses of Eastern Ontario, the barns and sheds set in the rolling hills of Prince Edward Island, but when I sat down to write about a book on the subject of old buildings, barns and sheds and lighthouses, I had to try and sort out the nature of that enthusiasm, to clarify some of the meanings of the past.

Architecture is a wonderfully mixed discipline, like Janus looking both ways, concerned with the new technologies of building, the usefulness of each design and also the old-fashioned appeal to the eye. A history of architecture must inevitably look at the development of all those elements. Working buildings like sheds and barns are those where the primary concern was the building's function. The techniques of building and the design were an expression of the techniques and materials of the time. The work was done by carpenters or local builders. That they appeal to our modern eye may be partly attributable to their distance from us in time.

Or not. There are a number of interesting aesthetic questions that arise about old buildings. Is the appeal of a group of old farm buildings merely a kind of nostalgia about the past? Partly that. Who would want to be a nineteenth-century pit sawyer producing the framing members for those old barns and lighthouses, arms aching from hours of working over your head, face full of sawdust? But there is more to it than that. Traditional carpenters, with quantities of excellent wood available, generally had some pride of workmanship and made functional buildings as the expression of a living craft. The barns and sheds and lighthouses have a certain purity of design because the only aesthetic element was the carpenter's sense of space. Anyone who's done any amount of blundering amateur carpentry knows that the greatest gift of a fine carpenter is the ability to imagine in three dimensions. One assumes that the old carpenters worked from memory, sketches, a vision in the mind's eye. Each had the wood, his tools and his eye, and the building went up. There would be little intrusion from the developments of fashion in such buildings. A history of housing is a history of fashion intruding on tradition; a history of farm buildings is the history of a tradition. With wood now expensive and generally of poor quality, most buildings, and especially functional buildings, are constructed from elements cheaply created by mass-production. Mass-production produces some beauty and inventiveness, but also much pedestrian ugliness. The beauty of the old places is real. I learned from watching my father about the beauty of wood and the discipline required to work with it.

I also learned that good craftsmanship was bad business. Not everyone was able to pay or prepared to pay for work that was done slowly, fastidiously, much of it by hand. It was easier to buy what was mass-produced. Craftsmanship was out of date.

3

Affordable luxury: a phrase I remember hearing on television in a commercial made for General Motors. Oxymoron is the technical word for that kind of expression, one that embodies an apparent contradiction, and the use of the device in a literary work is often an indication that the author is trying to suggest the complex depths of human emotional life.

But what to make of it in an economic setting? The contradictions involved in the idea of affordable luxury embody a lot of what is central to our current approach to the world. It is perhaps the great promise of consumer capitalism. A chicken in every pot and radicchio in every salad. Creative self-realization for everyone.

Luxury, traditionally, has been the preserve of a minority, the very rich, who could accumulate what was superfluous. The rest of society concentrated on achieving what was necessary to stay alive. The novels of Thomas Hardy show the passivity and simplicity of peasant life in the west country of England as late as the last decades of the nineteenth century. Other writers documented the narrow life of the industrial working class. And then we imagine the lives of the gentry, safe behind ranks of servants, eating, drinking, shooting, wearing fine clothes, seducing a porter or a chambermaid from time to time. Or we think of the Chinese mandarin practising calligraphy while the peasants laboured in fields and rice paddies.

This kind of picture has given luxury a bad name, while also making it seem rare and desirable, though as long as television shows pictures of starving children, the idea of superfluity is going to be suspect. Still, King Lear was not entirely wrong when, about to be deprived of his knights because he didn't need them, he argued that it's only what we have but do not need that makes us more than beasts. Most of what we call civilization is created by our adventures in the superfluous. Most of what we find in the great museums was created because it was wanted, not because it was needed. No-one has died for lack of a Botticelli.

What we need, of course, is very little. Food, water, shelter from the elements. A spartan existence is good for the body, and, some would say, good for the mind and soul. Certainly a puritan disdain for pleasure burnishes the will. One of the contradictions at the heart of capitalism is that it applauds the energetic endeavours of the will, the desire to control the self in order to make it the means of successful striving, while it produces vast quantities of goods that must be consumed if the machine is to go on.

It may be that modern technology is the arbiter of this contradiction. We need a new device—microwave, fax— but we are kept busy serving the device. It's been said before that the development of labour-saving devices has led to a substantial depletion of our leisure. Expenditure and restlessness go hand in hand. It is comprehensible, in ways admirable, the channelled simplicity of the keen will, the spartan life cluttered by devices, but the aesthetic arrives, offering its serene benediction, only with the truly superfluous.

In theory, modern capitalism provides increased choice, infinite variety: that is the ideology, but in fact choice is limited, doubly limited, first because, as I learned watching my father work, only uniformity (what can be mass-produced) is cheap, and second because it's in the nature of the system to turn choices into needs, and as soon as a need is felt, freedom vanishes, and with it any detached sense of beauty. Compulsion destroys charm.

Was luxury, among the rich, ever truly felt as luxurious? Was it only what Thorstein Veblen called "conspicuous consumption," a way of proving economic success? Perhaps we do not enjoy our possessions but only the power they symbolize. Luxury ought to involve an increase in pleasure, a multiplication of sensual delights. What pleasure did Imelda Marcos get from her vast collection of shoes? Did she take them in her hands each day, hold them up to the light, stroke the surface with her fingers? I doubt it. They were, more likely, a symbol of her authority, a bulwark against anxiety.

Pleasure is deeply innocent, but far fewer of us are capable of it than we would think. It means living in the transitory splendour of the present tense. Power, status, safety are what we really want from luxury, so what advertisers offer us is the moderately expensive masquerading as the more expensive, delusory symbols of position.

In fact, our needs are so few that most of us lead lives of luxury. A newspaper is a luxury. A change of clothes. When I decided to look, I found I owned seven or eight sweaters that I liked and was fond of wearing. Far more than I need. No doubt there are items, hand-worked, made of unusual materials, that cost the world and give delight by their excellence and rarity. They are true luxuries. Privacy is luxurious, and places of great beauty in which to enjoy it.

Epicurus, who said that the point of life was pleasure, aspired to a quiet life in a garden, with friends. Every spring, early, the chives come up, emerald green, and you can cook with them. There was the friend who knew where to find wild asparagus. Lyric, momentary, the best there is.

4

To live at the periphery and rarely read newspapers and current magazines has its advantages. I can be surprised. It was a fourteen-year-old who took us off to the movie, and knowing nothing of what we were to see except the title, I anticipated a teen flick. The films that turn up at the Charlottetown mall are, so far as I can tell, meant for people under 25 who would otherwise spend their leisure time shopping for clothes. I know there are other kinds of movies, but they come out of nowhere for a short run at the repertory cinema and then disappear back into the nowhere that created them.

Pleasantville, that's what it was called, this movie. I was startled when I looked around the audience to see I wasn't the only one with greying hair and a bald spot. Where were the teenagers? This was my first hint that I wasn't going to get what I was expecting.

Not long ago I read a review of a recent book about the philosophic sources of morality, and the reviewer pointed out that the purportedly 'natural' moral values that were being derived from *a priori* truths just happened to be the standards current in 1958. By the end of *Pleasantville*, I began to suspect that Gary Ross, who wrote, produced and directed it, had read that remark. The movie is about how an awkward teenage boy and his much more socially successful sister—"the slut thing" is how she describes her social life later on when she decides not to go back to it— who are left alone while their divorced mother goes off for a weekend with a lover, get themselves transposed, with a little assistance from Don Knotts as a weird TV-repairman,

89

into the black-and-white world of a nineteen-fifties television show called "Pleasantville." The dreamy and unhappy boy is addicted to reruns of the show, and at first the transposition seems like heaven to him, like hell to his sexy sister.

Now time-travel isn't new. It's a convention in lots of fiction for children these days, and in a way, in spite of those bald heads in the audience, *Pleasantville* is a teen movie, in which the two young people coming from the sophisticated present teach the black-and-white adults about the complications of real life. The sister Jennifer, in particular, is sexually experienced and becomes both Eve and serpent in the film's old-fashioned paradise. (Ross uses the apple image quite consciously.) She even teaches her TV mother how to masturbate. The TV parents are wonderfully cast and photographed, faces that are conventionally attractive in an old-fashioned way but raddled by vacuity.

The film starts off as a defence of things that are now identified with the sixties (at least if you remove the drugs from the old formula, sex, drugs and rock'n'roll), but for all its ironies at the expense of the naïve society that could enjoy "Father Knows Best," it is still a pretty innocent document. The sweet goof who runs the soda-fountain discovers modern art, everyone who has sex begins to appear in colour, and the city fathers mount a campaign against all this excessive liberty. There are moments of sudden resonance as when the stores begin to show signs in the window saying No Coloreds. Our young hero is summoned to a tribunal where innocence shows the other side of its face as his neighbours try to frighten him into agreeable compliance. There is real terror implicit in the revelation that if the infinitely repeatable gestures of black-and-white TV are rigid so is the world of black-and-white judgments when under threat. The movie appears to be suggesting that the political movement in the United

States that talks about "family values" is the expression of nothing authentic, not even a due respect for the difference of the past, but is rather an entrapment in fantasy, a surrender to illusion.

Another strong sequence in the film is the occasion when the TV mother, finding that sexual pleasure has made her turn coloured, is reassured by her son who covers her with monochrome makeup so she will still fit in. A little later, the proprietor of the local soda-fountain shows her the book of modern paintings he's come to love and in a gesture of gentle seduction, wipes off the makeup and reveals her in colour once again.

It's worth noting, of course, that the woman is the passive recipient of attention in each case.

At its best, *Pleasantville* proceeds by an appropriate filmic language, faces and places. The local barber-shop, the faces of the men in it, the look on the faces as they begin to grow militant against the threat of change, all these, presented in black and white, have echoes of something we might have seen in documentary footage from the American south in the early days of the civil-rights movement.

But finally no harm is done, honest self-expression wins out, and in a gesture toward the idea that personal development might be complex, Jennifer belatedly turns from black and white to colour only when she decides that she prefers reading a book to having obligatory sex with a dim-witted basketball star.

Lying somewhere behind the film is the modern debate about freedom and contentment. The terms were set by Dostoievsky in his parable of the Grand Inquisitor and developed by Aldous Huxley in *Brave New World*. Both suggest that human beings will prefer a commonplace contentment, free from anxiety, to the brighter but more dangerous delights of freedom. Dostoievsky's voice of

91

freedom is Christ; Huxley's is Shakespeare. Harold Bloom, in *Shakespeare and the Invention of the Human* argues that Shakespeare's greatest invention is the character of Falstaff, and that Falstaff, with his delight in life as a rich game, is the embodiment of freedom. That would make freedom the child of imagination, so that what must be escaped is not compulsion, but the feeling of being compelled.

Now *Pleasantville* is a very minor addition to this tradition—dismissed by many reviewers I'm told. It's as remarkable for its sly elisions as for its achievement, but as I walked out of the theatre, it struck me that a commercial American film based on an idea, a conscious exploration of ideology rather than a symptom of it, was an unexpected and worthwhile thing.

Gary Ross' *Pleasantville* is of its time, mostly preoccupied with sexual freedom as a part of personal fulfillment. Well, yes. That homosexuals no longer have to fear the police is an achievement. Women are somewhat less limited in their choices. There is a fine moment in the movie when the TV dad comes through the door and delivers his regular line, "Honey, I'm home." When his wife doesn't arrive, he can do nothing but repeat his line, confused and appalled. Such things don't happen. In the kitchen, he can't even remotely comprehend that his wife is gone and his meal uncooked. The stricken face of a man struggling with the wrong level of reality is funny and much more; we are, in fact, all sometimes at the wrong level of reality, living out a first-person fiction and trying to make others fit into it, appalled when they don't.

One of the elisions of the movie is the detail of the life of Jennifer here in the Coloured Nineties—My Life as a Slut—and it's possible that with regard to the role of women, the film offers only the choice between two stereotypes. Even if there is a high cost to liberation, a

92

portrayal of it wouldn't be edifying and would get the film a commercially dangerous R rating. And it would give aid and comfort to those family-values people. It's here that the movie, which is, after all, only a movie, fails to pay its way intellectually.

Still, we live, at the present time, in an era when men and women who inhabit homogeneous suburbs and shop in homogeneous malls are inveterate readers of books and magazines that offer them advice on self-realization and creative living. Everyone wants to be unique, but no-one wants to be weird. *Pleasantville* raises questions for that world.

The question of freedom, in the practical terms of day-to-day life, is a difficult one. Although we have a charter of rights that is said to protect liberty of the individual, and although we pay lip service to the idea of individual freedom, it's arguable that uniqueness is very rare and not much appreciated. We're not free, of course, unless we can choose to be like everybody else, but we're also not free unless we can at least imagine some other way of being.

In Passing

Boys in their teens are expected to be able to tell one make of car from another, and when I was a boy in my teens I could, more or less, but that was a while ago, and now when people ask me what kind of car I drive, I usually say grey. While I have the minimal knowledge of what goes on under the hood that comes from a lifetime of seeing things go wrong in there, I don't really care about the mechanism. Insofar as I have any manual dexterity, I prefer to expend it on wood, not metal. I have never learned to call kilometres "clicks," and my idea of a good time is for someone else to take the wheel.

You get the picture. I don't care about cars, and I use them more or less abusively until they go to the wreckers. On top of that, of course, I'm aware that they pollute the world in any number of ways, from the emission of exhaust to the piling up of worn tires and rusty metal. There was a time when, for family reasons, I made a lot of long trips through southern Ontario by car, but there wasn't much pleasure in it.

Imagine me, then, wheeling along a freeway somewhere in the United States and thinking that I'm having a pretty good time.

That's exactly what happened. I was alone in a small car for three days driving to Missouri and for three days driving back, and somewhere on the Cleveland bypass, in the rain, I realized that the sheer efficiency of the roads was a delight. I had driven past Syracuse, Rochester, Buffalo, Erie, and Cleveland, and I hadn't seen any of them. No doubt there are wonderful things to be learned about those cities, but I was going somewhere, and I was happy to be getting on with it, hurtling through space, crossing one state after another, chunks of the continent passing by, minute by minute, hour by hour.

At the beginning of the trip, the trees standing by the chill, misty St. Lawrence river showed only the first hint of opening buds. In Missouri, everything was thick and green and fresh. Summer.

The last time I'd driven a long distance alone was many years before, but it was spring that time too. Then I was driving north and east, leaving a place where the leaves were out and finding the remains of winter in the Gaspé and Newfoundland. Snow in the woods. A kind of geographical magic both times. Maybe to enjoy driving, it's best to be in no hurry. On the way south, I was going to visit a friend in St. Louis, but the visit was impulsive and undemanded. Given that, the miles of highway became an image of freedom, of sheer motion, of speed for its own sake, and as I drove along, following the code of signs that allowed me to miss the cities, I remembered how, sometimes, passing Toronto airport, I'll see the great silver planes arriving and departing, and think not of the stuffy cabins, the repeated announcements, but of the sheer wonder of the lift and thrust of the engines as the magic silver toys enter the sky.

In many ways, the modern world leaves me cold. I lack most of its gadgets. I've read George Grant on the effect of technology on our inmost being. But to live altogether outside the language of contemporary society requires a desperate rigidity, and the attempt may be a kind of sentimentality. Someone once said to me that I wouldn't use anything invented after 1958. Well, the car and the freeway were firmly in the world by then, so perhaps I was still within my own limits as I breezed toward Cincinnati in the early-morning sunlight. But even in a car there's more to life than a freeway, a package of gum and an atlas on the seat beside you, and I planned to turn off at

Cincinnati and take a day's detour through some of the back roads of Kentucky.

After a wrong turn, I got to see most of Cincinnati as well. A quiet place on a Sunday morning, and they still have that boulevard named after Pete Rose. For the rest of the day, it was the kind of driving I'd always admit to enjoying—country roads, small towns, a private museum in a place called Grant's Lick, a man selling what he called "a collage of junk" not far outside Lexington.

Do we travel seeking the exotic or only out of the need for motion? Styles become more and more the same across the world. In Lexington I had dinner in a patio restaurant—handsome young waiters in black and white—that might have been in Ottawa or Winnipeg.

I'm North American enough that there's a fascination in the road itself. I paid my visit in St. Louis and saw the city and had a good time, and then I was back on the blacktop on a Sunday morning, crossing the flatness of Indiana. A week or so later, back in Ontario, a tire would blow on Highway 401, but on the long roads of the midwest everything held together. I liked the flatness of those states, as I've always liked the prairies. I have a weakness for space, and in the American midwest, I discovered, there's a lot of it.

Unremarkable enough, perhaps, all this farmland, a few towns, fields that later in the year will be full of corn, but there's something about speed and the mere newness that makes it vivid. Space becomes time, the map rolls by. And then across the hazy morning air, like a vision, like one of the wonders of the modern world, I see the high towers of...Indianapolis.

The snow blows past the windows of the train as you look out into the almost monochrome landscape of northern New Brunswick, black shapes of the woods, white snow on the ground and along the branches, hints of dark green and brown as if a black and white photograph had been subtly touched up with colour. You pass a river, chunks of ice floating in the dark water. Now and then a ruined shack, or a highway, a village. You look back at the book you hold in your hand.

The train is the best way to travel if you can take the time, and as the slow journey goes on, the world outside the windows, the world of the people you meet on the train, and the world of the books you read all come together into a complex music of imagination. One summer evening on the edge of Newcastle, I looked out and saw a couple, working people by the look of them, standing in their yard to watch the train pass. They exist in some other dimension for me, as I, passing, do for them. A sign on the road says Station Street, and the name is somehow familiar. I searched my mind and came up with a title. *Nights Below Station Street*: those profligate encumbered lives created by David Adams Richards, the odder to call to mind when I found myself reading Henry James.

A trip just before Christmas. On the way west through New Brunswick, Quebec and Ontario, I was reading Timothy Findley's novel *The Piano Man's Daughter*. Toronto was my destination, and the streets of the city were laid out in front of me in his words. The man in the seat next to me had been a Toronto cab driver for 30 years, though he was now living in Nova Scotia and doing woodwork, and we talked about the old suburban train stations. I can remember from childhood a St. Clair Avenue station where the train, which had earlier set off from downtown, picked up passengers before continuing northwest. We may have been going to visit my grandfather or maybe to a summer cottage when we caught the train there one bright morning. I think my mother bought me a new book to keep me amused during the trip. Most of *The Piano Man's Daughter* takes place before I was born, but the way the city was shaped by streetcars and how southern Ontario was held together by trains was magically familiar. Findley's family chronicle, like a train trip through a landscape you love, makes the familiar exotic, and interrupted by food and sleep and conversation with strangers, it carried me to Toronto, where I got off the train for a family reunion of my own.

You walk the streets of the Annex, take the streetcar to Cabbagetown, have lunch in Kingston between trains, move on and find yourself walking across the bridges between Hull and Ottawa, crossing from one province to another in the bitter cold. In Hull, I picked up a copy of Ray Conlogue's *Impossible Nation, The Longing for Homeland in Canada and Quebec*, a book that has its roots in the experience of arriving in Montreal to live and work and attempting to see with clear eyes, the sheer differentness of a different culture speaking a different language. (Does that bridge across the Ottawa lead from province to province or country to country?) I had moved to Montreal around the same time as Conlogue, and had an experience a little like his. Now, arriving back on a visit, I went to my old neighbourhood, the French streets east of the mountain, to do some shopping, and it was, as always, another world.

The train to the east leaves Montreal in the evening, and in winter, you travel through Quebec in darkness. At Lévis, the bright lights of Quebec City on the steep heights across the river. Then you sleep and wake, sleep and wake, through Gaspé and into New Brunswick. By now I was reading *White Madness*, a collection of Alden Nowlan's columns for the *St. John Telegraph-Journal*, and it was Christmas Eve.

Alden Nowlan died in 1983, and fifteen years later, the publishers were having trouble getting people to notice his book. Public memory is short. "I suppose I should know who he is," one young librarian said. A voice from the past: I didn't know Alden well, but it was back in 1970 that I first met him, and he always embodied a certain old-fashioned respect for the way things are. The voice in the newspaper columns is very much his own, but the level of irony, the way he played with the events of ordinary life reminded me of books I read in the nineteen-fifties. He had something of the manner of Stephen Leacock, or what I could remember of Robert Benchley, or Thurber perhaps, or the Robertson Davies of the Marchbanks books, which also began as newspaper columns. In the work of those writers, there is no sense that one needs to speak of deep matters, of great issues, or deep personal pain. Nowlan was a master of the decorum of small things. By comparison, I thought as the train rolled on, how fraught and self-indulgent a lot of contemporary essays are. Axes are ground to a fine edge and beyond. Picking sides is everyone's favourite athletic activity.

Reading about banking and birthdays, cats and licorice, I look out the train window. We've stopped somewhere, and families are greeting each other on the platform. A mother and daughter walk arm-in-arm while father and son-in-law follow behind working at conversation. It is the accepted wisdom that we are the children of revolution, that everything has been transformed, for the better or for the worse, but when you sit in a train that has run on more or less the same tracks through more or less the same towns for a hundred years or so, and you see the bustle of coming and going, you think for a moment that

99

nothing much has changed.

Look back to the book. Nowlan is writing about some old New Brunswick school readers that he's been looking at. "In a curious kind of way," he says, "the Canadian outlook may have been more cosmopolitan and less colonial in 1898 than it is today. I'm not sure that that's true, but it's a thought that occurred to me as I examined this old schoolbook." A different reading, that is, of past and present, a useful corrective in a world where the word conservative has lost its meaning or been hijacked by what my old friend David Lewis Stein calls "the Leninists of the right."

Good books encourage you to take a second look. As I sat in the train seeing the small towns of New Brunswick and the people who lived in them, all I could think was how little some things alter. On an earlier trip, going west, I met Newfoundlanders who were going west to look for work in Alberta. The young men sitting behind me on this trip were back for a visit from a place they were working in BC. Change, sure enough, but there's no sense that these people aspire to a new kind of life. They want a job and go where the work is, as their fathers did, as my father did.

Nowlan has a comic essay about how he can no longer get out of Fredericton by train. Fly or stay home. That's true in a lot of places, where the old stations are mouldering. Is that inevitable change or the illusion of change? Perhaps those who spend half their life in the air and wired lose track of those of us on the ground, still moving pretty slowly, and so they invent those new rules by which you have to have particular educational requirements in order to be a school janitor. Every politician and journalist should be required at least once a year to take a long train ride through the country. We are still out there on foot in the snow.

Noon on 24 December and the Moncton railway station
was crowded. Christmas travellers who had just got off the
train after a night and morning moving through the winter landscapes of Quebec and northern New Brunswick,
stopping at small towns lost in the snow, were being
greeted by those who had come to pick them up, groups
sorting hand luggage and parcels, waiting for the wagons
of baggage now being unloaded to be brought along the
platform to the baggage-room just beside the ticket
counter. There was no-one to meet me here in Moncton,
and my luggage would be transferred to the Charlottetown bus that arrived later on. I had nothing to do but
watch the little scenes from provincial life, the tall man in
breeches and boots, a fur hat, a noticeable German accent,
something from a Lehar operetta or *The Sound of Music*, a
bit officious, a bit flustered as he greeted a young woman
almost as tall as he was, who might perhaps have been his
granddaughter.

Just by where I was sitting, in a corner near the telephones and washrooms, under a bronze plaque with a date
in the nineteen-thirties commemorating a former presi-
dent of the railroad, were two young women, with bags
and attendant lords, one girl pale and quiet, the other full
of attitude and complaint. Contemporary rules would tell
me that these were not girls, that girls become young
women at puberty or before, but life and language resist
such simplicities; the recently matured, perfectly realized
young bodies did not emit the message of an adult engagement with life. The attendant lords were bowing and
retreating, having done their duty in getting the girls off
the train, and when the first rush at the telephones was
over, one of the young women (let's call her that this
time—another half-truth) made a call, which immediately

became a loud and dramatic scene.

"Duane, I've been up the whole fucking night on the train. There was no seat on the plane and it cost me $35 to get to the station...." She was wearing black trousers, boots with leather heels which she stamped loudly in a display of frustration, and then she was in tears, her voice whining for sympathy easily heard all the way across the room. "I called you from the airport, I did, and I called your cell phone...I know...I know...I didn't know I wasn't going to get on the plane...I didn't get any fucking sleep at all...."

The voice had a raucous edge and she had no sense of who might be overhearing or a theatrical pleasure in being heard. Look at me: I have a perfect little body in tight black trousers and am the centre of the world. Now she was admitting repentantly that she could have tried harder to phone and then she was hanging up, and sniffing and sobbing, crossed from the phones to concealment in the women's washroom, the heels cracking against the station floor, and the pale girl followed her to offer comfort. They were both young and pretty, and I was sitting in the middle of their lives, waiting for a bus. There was something she'd said about a phone number where she didn't want to call Duane. Where he was at work. Or perhaps Duane was married. No probably not, for we had all heard how he had been up all night waiting for her call.

The tall aristocratic German in his Lehar costume had vanished, and the long lineup at the baggage-room door began to dissipate. At the phones, a man speaking French, making his arrangements. Now the girl in the black pants was talking to a young man who might have been Indian perhaps, or from the Middle East, and who might or might not be someone she knew. Probably she'd met him on the train. He listened politely but had nothing to say in response to her stream of confessions and complaints.

Then the baggage line cleared, and the crowd dissipated, and here she was in tears again, on her way back from the baggage-room, her heels beating their dramatic percussion across the floor.

"They lost my fucking parcel...." The complaints rattled on and the young man listened in silence. By now the other young woman, the pale one, had disappeared. Not a friend, as I had thought at first, but only another acquaintance from the train, drawn in by the magnetic pull of so much desire. The rage of a difficult child, hunger, the need to make things happen. The girl had good features, a certain air of style to go with her smoky voice and street-corner brashness. Small and neatly built. The pants were tight, but she was able to wear tight pants, and there was nothing cheap about the look, the mauve shirt, the short jacket. She was complaining now about the clubs back here in the Maritimes, and I wondered what she did in Toronto, where she worked, whether in a clothing store where she cleaned up her talk. Or could she be at school somewhere? She was a fighter, brought up to rebellion and self-pity. She was the kind of girl who got beaten up or murdered, and some tight-assed neighbour would say she deserved it.

The waiting-room was almost empty now, a handful of people still waiting for the bus or belated rides. I'd gone across to the mall to get a sandwich, and sat eating it. Soon there would be no-one but the bus passengers to the Island. A bulky young couple with many bags was still there, and the woman, obviously a kind soul, went to the little battler and asked about her lost parcel. I didn't hear the beginning of the story, but then they were crossing the room together, and the girl was complaining about the railroad staff, and the other woman was agreeing, yes she had travelled alone too and men were always coming onto you, and then somehow the girl was explaining that she had spent the night smoking up in the dome car with a man (he was 25 years old, she said, though the significance wasn't clear, maybe that he was in her terms an older man) who had paid her to spend the night there with him.

"We didn't do anything, but I had a better time than with lots of guys I've gone out with, and I ended up with $25 and some shit."

Would Duane have a pretty good idea of why she didn't sleep all night on the train? Maybe not. The bulky woman seemed able to handle the shift of gears, and soon enough she and her man loaded themselves with their many bags and went out the door, a little like two missionaries setting off into the jungle, I thought, and the younger woman, calm enough now, the tears and rage left behind like some boring guy you only wanted to forget, went out for a smoke. I thought maybe she was waiting for the bus to the island, but when the bus left, over an hour later, she was still sitting outside, on her suitcase, perfectly patient, waiting for whatever was going to happen next. Duane must be coming to pick her up in spite of his anger. Probably they'd have another fight. Why did I suppose that men were there in her life as background, supporting players, that she didn't much like sex?

If she hadn't been determined to take off to Toronto, she might have stayed somewhere, married, smacked her kids a lot, broken up with her husband, maybe ended up with only booze and smokes for company. Maybe that's what she would go back to, that or something like it. You never knew for sure what went on behind the drawn blinds of another face, whether what was advertised on the marquee was really the movie that was playing. She offered her privacy in bleeding chunks and then retreated into time. I knew I would never see her again, and I couldn't imagine her future. As the bus went over the long bridge to PEI in the late afternoon, the sky and the water were astonishing, the winter sky pale blue and green and white in the far distance, while the water was vivid emerald, with a long snake of floating chunks of ice leading off to the luminous, mysterious horizon.

Seven Thoughts About The Hidden

I: THE HIDDEN KING

It all began with the Princess of Wales, some time before her sudden death and the huge public response. She was on television telling her story, and there in the *Globe and Mail* the next day, Michael Valpy was defending the idea of the monarchy against all the silliness. "The monarchy," he said, "is the personification of a people's freedom."

Years ago I astonished a friend, born in the United States, by offering a defence of the monarchy as a way of embodying the state in a single person who reigns, but doesn't rule. The state, of course, is a sort of fiction, and in ways so is the king or queen. How exactly does the queen reign? Well, by representing something, and just possibly, in a moment of emergency, being an expression of political tradition through moral force. Apparently the King of Denmark did not in fact put on a yellow star when the Danish Jews were ordered to wear one, but the often-heard story that he did embodies the argument about moral force. We want to believe in something that is the image of a potential best self, that stands beyond our weaknesses. Politicians are meant to sway in the wind of popular approval and disapproval. That's their calling, but our best traditions should stand beyond that.

In 1940, France found itself facing a military defeat that became a crisis of the legitimacy of the Third Republic. Lacking a monarch, they turned to an old soldier, one of the marshalls of France, Marshall Pétain, with consequences we all know. Pétain felt that he was embodying and defending France in an emergency, but the result was the humiliation of his country.

There are many good and bad things about the American system of government, but the one that has always

106

struck me as the worst is that the symbolic head of state is an elected politician. It's no wonder so many of them have got assassinated. The emotional accretions to that political error led to the situation where most of the world found the American fuss and turbulence over Bill Clinton's sex life ineffably comic.

Constitutional monarchy—symbolic monarchy we might call it—may seem like a good idea, but events surrounding the British throne have brought the idea into question. The need of the press for fodder and the fact that the Princess of Wales was a pretty girl turned her into a phenomenon of modern journalism, with bad effects on almost everyone. Constitutional monarchs are meant to be symbols, not celebrities.

As I was thinking about that problem I remembered something in a volume of Pierre Berton's autobiography. Berton's first book was about the monarchy, in fact about the Royal Tour in the nineteen-fifties. While he was working on the book, he was reading in *The Golden Bough* Sir James Frazer's remarks about sacred kings and priests. Berton talked about observing the Queen, the way in which her behaviour was circumscribed by certain proprieties because of her symbolic role. She could not be seen eating an apple because it might seem too ordinary, something less that royal.

Now we get to know everything. "There's such divinity doth hedge a king..." Hamlet said. Well, maybe.

Then it came to me. What we need, I decided, is a secret monarch, a queen let's say, one who reigns, who has the moral power to reveal her identity in a crisis and act as the present one or her representative might act, who might have a royal name—Queen Jane, Queen Marie—sign documents with that name and in the meantime go about her business, unknown to anyone, as plain old Gail Smithers, or Margaret Atwood or k.d. lang—we might want someone who had shown a certain level of public responsibility—but no-one would know. Anyone you met on the street might be the queen. Or the king. When the reigning one died, we could still have a splendid state funeral.

A ridiculous idea? Of course it's a ridiculous idea, but that doesn't make it wrong. The greatest single corruption in our society is probably the religion of celebrity, and to keep a monarch immune from that is to offer true reverence to the symbolism of the office, to the personification of the people. The hidden king would move among us, potent but unknown.

2: THE HIDDEN TEACHERS

Steiner, Tomberg, Blavatsky. Christian Mystery Teachings in this stream are currently being dictated to us by the advanced elder brothers of humanity. Available in pamphlet form. Write or fax for catalog and sample subjects....

The advanced elder brothers of humanity: once you begin thinking about hidden kings, they pop up everywhere. A magazine that describes itself as *A Journal of the Western Inner Traditions* will tell you about a persistent legend that in some hidden location there are groups of persons with exceptional powers and highly developed consciousness. It says they are known variously as the Hierarchy of Adepts, or The Masters.

The essential thing about these figures is that they possess some kind of secret knowledge, an understanding of things into which others can't penetrate, though these elder brothers have the habit of offering this occult wisdom to a few outsiders, who then, I suppose, become insiders. One of those who was offered a look in was the famous Mme Blavatsky, the founder of Theosophy, a movement that had a large following earlier in this century and probably still has some adherents. Apparently Mme Blavatsky had spiritual teachers, whether these teachers were spiritual existences or whether she mythologized certain actual Indian gurus isn't clear.

I don't know if anyone studies Mme Blavatsky any more, but the idea that there are mysterious teachers with secret wisdom hasn't died out. Look at all those books about angels, the stories of reincarnation. As traditional authority has lost its magic, there has developed a kind of free-floating desire for something to replace it, and all manner of myths and legends have been brought into play.

Everything from angels to the hierophantic figures of science-fiction, the myth of the wise beings who watch us from flying saucers, who will rescue us in an emergency. There's something called channelling that brings in mysterious voices.

Most of this kind of thinking strikes me as naïve and irresponsible. These are myths that require no obvious discipline. One waits for the extraterrestrials to land and get us out of our present mess. They are, of course, figures of parental authority, and the desire to believe in such hidden masters is a version of the infantile desire for safety. Even a famous children's story knows better.

3: THE HIDDEN WIZARD

"Where are you all going?"

"To the Emerald City," said Dorothy, "to see the Great Oz."

"Oh, indeed!" exclaimed the man. "Are you sure that Oz will see you?"

"Why not?" she replied.

"Why it is said that he never lets anyone come into his presence. I have been to the Emerald City many times, and it is a beautiful and wonderful place; but I have never been permitted to see the Great Oz, nor do I know of any living person who has seen him."

"Does he never go out?" asked the Scarecrow.

"Never. He sits day after day in the great throne-room of his palace, and even those who wait upon him do not see him face to face."

"What is he like?" said the girl.

"That is hard to tell," said the man thoughtfully. "You see Oz is a great Wizard, and can take on any form he wishes. So some say he looks like a bird; and some say he looks like an elephant; and some say he looks like a cat. To others he appears as a beautiful fairy or a brownie, or in any form that pleases him. But who the real Oz is, when he is in his own form, no living person can tell."

This great Wizard—who is to give the Scarecrow brains, the Tin Woodman a heart, the Lion courage, and to send Dorothy back to Kansas—is another version of the wise mentor, a projection of our need whose power is related to his hiddenness. But of course this is a comic version of the story. Dorothy and her companions come into the throne-room of the Great Oz.

Of course each of them expected to see the Wizard in the shape he had taken before, and all were greatly surprised when they looked about and saw no-one at all in the room. They kept close to the door and closer to one another, for the stillness of the empty room was more dreadful than any of the forms they had seen Oz take.

Presently they heard a voice, seeming to come from somewhere near the top of the great dome, and it said solemnly:

"I am Oz, the Great and Terrible. Why do you seek me?"

They looked again in every part of the room, and then seeing no-one, Dorothy asked, "Where are you?"

"I am everywhere," answered the Voice, "but to the eyes of common mortals I am invisible."

Once again the magic figure is hidden, but in L. Frank Baum's classic little book, the hidden is revealed.

"You must keep your promises to us!" exclaimed Dorothy.

The Lion thought it might be well to frighten the Wizard, so he gave a large loud roar which was so fierce and dreadful that Toto jumped away from him in alarm and tipped over the screen that stood in the corner. As it fell with a crash they looked that way, and the next moment all of them were filled with wonder. For they saw, standing in just the spot the screen had hidden, a little old man with a bald head and a wrinkled face, who seemed to be as much surprised as they were.

So there you have it—at least in the comic version. Projection and illusion end in laughter. The hidden power, the source of magic, is only a very ordinary creature, a trickster.

4: THE HIDDEN ANSWERS

In clapping both hands a sound is heard. What is the sound of the one hand?

Wu-tsu said, "It is like a buffalo that passes through a latticed window. Its head, horns and all four legs pass through. Why can't its tail pass through as well?

What is your original face, before your mother and father were born?

Perhaps behind it all there is not a funny little man, but nothing at all. The riddles posed by the masters of Zen Buddhism were meant to lead away from consequential thought and toward the contemplation of being. Which means the contemplation of non-being. Of nothing. The student was led to search life for the hidden and both to find it and not find it. To discover a mystery, but not one that can be explained, a mystery that is both absolute and transparent. William Blake talked about finding a world in a grain of sand.

What the Zen master did was to ask questions. But these weren't questions that had answers in the ordinary sense of that word. The wisdom was in seeing the question as both significant and absurd. The hidden remained hidden, though it gave a spiritual energy to the overt. In his first book on the Bible, Northrop Frye has something interesting to say about questions and answers. "To answer a question," he says, "is to consolidate the mental level on which the question is asked." The answer is less a solution than a form of reassurance.

5: THE HIDDEN SAINTS

This was in Cracow in the days of Rabbenu Moses Isserls. Someone told the King of Poland that as the descendent of the Persian King he was entitled to a sum of money, money that Haman had promised to him, but which he had not paid, because he had been robbed of it by the Jews. So the Polish King ordered the Jews of Cracow to pay him an enormous sum of money. If they didn't pay it right away, they would be subjected to a terrible persecution. What were they to do? After long fasting, Rabbenu Isserls told his congregation to go to Chaim the tailor who was living on the edge of town, and to ask him to use his supernatural powers to save them.

"Me?" said Chaim, "I have no such powers. I can do nothing."
But they insisted and he promised to go to the King.
The next morning he went to the palace. He passed by the
guards. They didn't notice him. He went right into the King's
private cabinet and asked him to sign a document revoking his
order. The King grew angry and went quickly to the door to chide
the guards for having admitted this ragged Jew.
But as he opened the door, he stepped into space and found
himself in a desert. He wandered about for a whole day and only
in the evening, he met a poor man who offered him a piece of dry
bread and showed him where to shelter in a cave. For a year the
King lived in his cave, on dry bread, dressed like a beggar. At
the end of the year, the poor man offered him work as a wood-
cutter, with better wages if he would sign a document. The king
agreed. And so it went on. His trials lasted for two more years,
and finally he became a sailor, and he was shipwrecked at
Cracow.
And just then he woke to discover that this three years had
only lasted fifteen minutes by the clock. But he kept the agreement
that he had signed in his dream and so great misfortune to the
Jews of Cracow was warded off by poor ragged Chaim the tailor.

In that old Jewish legend, Chaim the tailor is one of the
lamed-vovniks, the 36 hidden saints. The legend has it
that in every generation there are 36 secret saints, through
whose piety the world exists. They are humble people who
hide their sanctity, and even they themselves may not
know that they are among the 36. Once his act is com-
pleted, the lamed-vovnik vanishes back into anonymity.

This legend evokes my vision of the hidden king, and
so vividly that I suspect I must have heard it and tucked it
away among the things that are lost but not forgotten. I
had no conscious memory of the legend of the 36 until it
was mentioned to me by a friend and I did some research,
but it is a legend of great moral beauty. Look around you,

and anyone you see might be a secret saint. To ponder the legend leads us to think how little we know about the inner lives of others, how much hidden goodness there may be in the world. If Zen suggests the presence of inapprehensible meaning, the legend of the lamed-vovniks suggests the presence of inapprehensible goodness.

6: THE HIDDEN CHILD

And the woman conceived and bare a son: and when she saw him that he was a goodly child, she hid him three months. And when she could no longer hide him, she took for him an ark of bulrushes and daubed it with slime and with pitch, and put the child therein; and she laid it in the flags by the river's brink....

The story of the child Moses, after Pharaoh has decreed that the firstborn of every Israelite family shall die. He is rescued from the reeds by Pharaoh's daughter and raised in Pharaoh's house, and becomes the great leader of his people. Elements of the story of the birth of Jesus are parallel, the child laid in a manger, then taken away to hiding in Egypt to avoid Herod, whose murderous jealousy is parallel to that of Pharaoh. In our own time, the Buddhists of Tibet still seek the new Dalai Lama or Pathet Lama among the children of ordinary people. They must search diligently to find the one who is the reincarnation of an earlier Buddha.

If this seems a long way from the secret king, consider the events surrounding the search for a new Pathet Lama. The communist party, which had suppressed the traditional practice of seeking a new lama, for some reason allowed the search for a new Pathet Lama to begin, but then decided that they had to be in control of the process, and when the list of candidates was somehow sent out of the country to the Dalai Lama in exile who chose a six-year old boy, the Chinese government objected and made the monks start over with a new list from which the lama was to be chosen by lot.

Chance is better than inspiration. A very modern conclusion, but the story is a perfect example of the way that power and symbolism overlap. Many people have observed that the embalmed figures of Mao and Lenin and—once upon a time—Stalin, were holy objects. It may be that nothing can entirely take away the human need to find images of the sacred, but given the impulse of human beings toward many forms of tyranny, the sacred should be as far beyond us as possible. Instead of ruining the life of a pretty, rather vapid young woman, we are better to place the royal, the divine, the sacred, safely beyond our reach. We may think that Moses and Jesus are the figures we revere, but Herod and Pharaoh get a lot of votes in most elections.

7: THE HIDDEN GOD

It happens in the same way spiritually when within our hearts we desire to know God himself. For even if a man is deeply versed in the understanding and knowledge of all spiritual things ever created, he can never by such understanding come to know an uncreated spiritual thing...which is none else than God.

What if even God is hidden? Pascal says somewhere, "Every religion which does not affirm that God is hidden is not true.... *Vere tu es deus absconditus.*" There is a whole kind of theology that is based on that possibility, usually called apophatic or negative theology. The reality of a god, such a theology would say, is beyond any merely human statement. We can only say what God is not—not limited, not mortal, not visible. The source of much of this tradition is the writer who's known as Pseudo-Dionysus the Areopagite. "The Deity is far beyond every manifestation of being and life," he says. And this, "God is in no way like the things that have being, and we have no knowledge at all of his incomprehensible and ineffable transcendence and invisibility."

Many conceptions of deity are projections of human weaknesses and desires. God is a parental figure on whom we project our need for comfort and support. Or God is a wrathful figure who justifies our own rage. Fundamentalists may see the first as a liberal heresy. Most liberals will see the second as a particular failing of fundamentalists. Belief in a willful God allows willful human conduct. It's a common perception that wars of religion have been among the cruelest and bloodiest in the history of the world. And they are still among us.

I found some of what I've quoted about apophatic theology in a book by Jaroslav Pelikan called *The Melody of Theology*. The book is organized in short alphabetical sections, and so, by reason of a Greek prefix, apophatic theology comes next to agnosticism and atheism, and Pelikan says of it, "In recent times, apophatic theology has shown signs of becoming trendy, sometimes as a cloak for an agnostic outlook that denies the reality of revelation and incarnation altogether."

There are worse things than believing that we do not know. Atheism—which might be called the fundamentalism of science—sometimes shows the same lack of humility and imagination as most fundamentalism. The idea of a possible but hidden god at least allows for a way of thinking that is modest and yet capacious. Its weakness, of course, is that it can represent mere syncretism, an eclectic looking around for the good bits, religious window-shopping. It requires the constant acknowledgment that beyond our metaphors is death, that being is only a temporary evasion of the longer and greater unbeing.

As in politics, liberalism may be betrayed by its own hopes. We easily forget that we do not have democracy because men are good, but because they are not. The acknowledgment that we are vulgar, murderous, greedy, makes an easy eclecticism hollow.

These are hard matters. It was after the Holocaust that rabbinical thinkers had to begin to ask themselves where God was in Auschwitz. He had gone away. He had hidden his face. What is equally terrible is that the murder of the Jews can only be thought of as a religious act. In some places, greedy men gained by it, but largely it was performed as an act of belief. A duty of hate. It was done because it was believed to be right. An atheist state had become a god, and that god demanded purification of the temple.

Better to try to think of the inapprehensible, knowing that it will stay hidden. That offers at least a certain humility.

EPILOGUE

The function of the king is primarily to represent, for his subjects, the unity of their society in an individual form. Even yet Elizabeth II can draw crowds wherever she appears, not because there is anything remarkable about her appearance, but because she dramatizes the metaphor of society as a single 'body.'

That's a quotation from Northrop Frye. Sometimes the right book falls into your hands at the right time. It was my own intuition that there was a crucial link of political and religious metaphors, and that started me on this process of thought. Then as I was in the process of working it out, I began rereading Frye's book on the Bible, *The Great Code*, and I came on a section on what he calls "the royal metaphor." What he is talking about is all those forms of speech and action where our individuality is seen as a part of something larger.

Traditionally the messiah is a figure that will knit us all in one. The Christian statement of this is, "we are all members of one body." This is both a comforting and a deeply dangerous metaphor. Unified societies are often totalitarian societies. There is a kind of wisdom in the traditional Jewish contention that the messiah is still to come—someday—and the effect of abandoning this patient waiting, turning the state of Israel into a messianic kingdom, is all too evident.

I once found myself in a small courthouse, observing a jury trial, and there was a moment I have never forgotten. I come back to it often. At the beginning of the trial, the judge spoke to the jury in a standard form of words. Of the defendant he said, "he has put himself upon his country, which country you are."

There it is, Frye's royal metaphor, but without the trappings of traditional or specious royalty. The jury represents the country while at the same time being ordinary people who will disappear after the trial into the anonymous ordinary life. They were hidden, they will be hidden, and yet they embody, temporarily, all of what we are. That is the reason that they must not be interviewed after the trial, that they must not discuss their deliberations. They must be kept safe from the great corruption, celebrity. Better that they be unknown. Only in that way can we understand that the royal metaphor is a fiction that must be honoured yet known as a fiction.

The king, the secret saints, the messiah, all may be thought of as hidden among us. They are meet objects of our contemplation. But they must never be found.

Looking and Listening

I

Sometimes I think of myself as a reactionary, suspicious of the contrivances of the modern world, but I remember walking down a new street in a new suburb of Toronto and watching men finishing up the last bits of work on an apartment building and realizing there's one element of the modern that I have always loved: the prevalence of glass, those wide transparent apartment walls, rooms where you can stand in the sky.

They are magical things, windows, and floor-to-ceiling windows are like walls of light. I don't know just when they began to be used. The first I remember were in apartment buildings in Toronto in the late fifties. Before that, I had only seen plate-glass in the windows of stores.

(Another kind of magic. Going downtown at Christmas to see the windows of Eaton's and Simpson's, a world of fantasy behind glass.)

There's also the fascinating difference between looking out and looking in. Can anyone, walking down a street at night, resist a glance into the lighted windows? There on the other side is...what? Human life as it might be in a book or film, silent, familiar and alien. Men and women going about their business, and the one who watches is outside, untouched, unknown, omnipotent. As solitary as a god. The wall of glass between us and those lives is startling and new. Every moment is a part of the story. The voyeur is trapped by that combination of intimacy and distance, while most of us pass by, enlivened by the lyric moment.

If the life glimpsed through an uncurtained window offers the world of reality become, for a moment, fantastic, the vision through a display window offers a fantasy tempting you to realize it. Come in, it says, and you too can be put on display, perfected.

Glass severs the eye from the hand and concentrates one part of our brain. There is something in the fact of transparency that shapes and alters our perceptions. Even a ten-inch window-pane or a department-store wine-glass can perform the trick. The awareness of what can be seen but not touched enforces an intense and detached knowing. Clear glass is an object lesson in the nature of the aesthetic.

As I was thinking about this, sitting in a small restaurant, I looked out the window, and beyond it, in a courtyard, a woman popped out of her shop to alter the sign on her door from Open to Closed. With the window between us, her action was framed. It became part of an untold story.

Glass: the window, the lens, the mirror, all the things that alter our way of seeing. The most magical, the most powerful of these is the window. The mirror is the focus of functional or neurotic self-love. The lens is pragmatic and imperative. We take a picture, or we analyze by microscope or telescope. The window is more ambiguous in its relationship to light. Caught at a certain angle, it may be a mirror; in its ability to focus perception it's not unlike a lens; and yet it has a neutral, practical function: to allow in the light by which we carry on our lives.

As I write this, there is a window above me, to my left, and another at my level, further off, to the right. If I look left, I see part of a tree, a telephone line, a grey sky. If I look right, I see, beyond the wild-grape vines that cover half the glass, the corner of a building, and beyond that, the corner of another. Simple enough things, but framed by the window and separated from me by a transparent sheet of glass, they become pictures.

Although in the last hundred years a lot of artists have created works that question the convention, much of the history of western art is the history of a scene contained within a flat rectangle, a window on the world.

(Part of the fascination of any trip by bus or train is that the passing landscape is continually framed by the moving window of the vehicle, creating a kind of movie, all setting and little plot, an experience of landscape radically different from standing in the middle of its uncontained plenitude.)

The window is part of a wall, and yet it is a point of access to the light beyond. In front of me is a print of a seventeenth-century Dutch painting, an interior by an artist named Pieter Janssens. In a large room with a patterned floor a woman is reading a book. Behind her is a rather stiffly painted dog, above her a mirror reflecting the floor and above the mirror are two windows, full of daylight. Patches of light from the windows fall on the floor and wall of the room, and one of them is reflected in such a way that it casts the shadow of a chair on the wall. To the left is an open door and beyond that is a room where a man stands, and beyond the man, there is another window.

A conventional enough painting of the period, without the brilliance of Vermeer, and yet there is a typical and intriguing tension created by the windows, and perhaps by the door as well. Easy enough to say that this picture is a study of light, and a commonplace of criticism, but the particular tension here is between the solid substantial interior, and the hint of what is beyond. The freedom and energy of light is located and questioned by the transparent wall that is the window. There is the here, and there is the beyond, not the gradual beyond of the perspective vista, or the mysterious beyond of chiaroscuro, but the teasing haunted beyond of the glass window. The transcendent that can be seen but never touched.

Windows create all manner of mysteries. As I write this, I am in a house at the top of a small hill. The win-

dows face east and west. Below me on the hill is an apartment building with plate-glass windows. Sometimes the
sunset is reflected there. Once I looked out a west window
at a grey cloudy sky and then looked east to see a contra-
dictory version, a brilliant sunset, reflected back at me.
Not only in physics is light an absolute. It is the key to
all sorts of periodic processes in living creatures. Glass
plays with light as thought plays with being: separation,
reflection, refraction, all are ways of provoking the eye to
awareness.

There's another part to it as well. I have a scar on my
left hand from an accident during the annual—though
increasingly outdated—adventure of putting on storm
windows. Looking at the scar, remembering the sudden
crash, the blood, I wonder if one element in the magic of
glass is the hidden knowledge of its fragility. It stands
between us and what is out there, and yet we know how
easily and dangerously it can shatter, severing flesh, leaving us bare to the world.

2

Listen. What do you hear? I can hear the very quiet
chirping of a bird, and someone crashing pieces of wood
and metal a block or so away. And of course the offensive
(if noticed) noise of the machine on which I'm composing
this, but I don't notice it, not really. It's an habitual thing
that goes with writing. Behind or beyond these noises,
there is an inner background, the words of this sentence as
they are imagined, and some piece of music (*Laudamus te,
benedicimus te*). I can't remember who wrote it.

Sounds are multiple, overlaid in odd perspectives,
loaded with feeling. Every sense has its place in our personal and social connections to the world, but sound is

122

particularly fascinating, how we shape it and it shapes us.

More than any other sense, sound affects the borderline where one person meets another. Good and bad smells are largely involuntary. Touch is at the extreme of aggressiveness or intimacy. Sight is omnipresent, functional, fluid. If a sight is unpleasant, you can avert your eyes. Impossible to avert your ears. If someone on the patio next door decides to turn a tape player up to its highest level, I am assaulted. If someone stops at a red light with a car radio blaring, I can't escape the noise.

Sound has the power of touch, but without the set of conventions that go along with physical contact. Strangers who would never consider hitting me feel perfectly free to attack me with loud noises. Sound invades our space even when it comes from a distance.

A while back, I began to be aware of an idiosyncrasy about sound and space. If I am listening to music and someone walks into the room, even if I have no intention of starting a conversation and even if the music is something the other person is likely to enjoy, I have to turn down the volume or even turn it off. I can't explain this, but the need is compelling. The other person takes up a certain amount of psychic space and the music a certain amount, and one or the other must be adjusted.

There are those people who can carry on a serious conversation with the television set on. Not me. At least one of my children habitually did homework, and did it perfectly well, while watching TV. Then there was the day I met an old friend in the library. He was getting some light reading, books to be read while he watched TV.

In all these cases, it's the sound that prevents my concentration. Turn off the sound and the TV virtually ceases to exist. I could tell myself that this is merely a symptom of a rigid and linear personality, a mind that must have the level of stimuli firmly in order. Perhaps.

However I can dodge through a crowded art gallery and get what I want. The visual confusion doesn't cause a problem.

I know there are writers who like to work with music playing. Unthinkable. I can handle quite a lot of random background noise (people are laughing and chatting 50 feet away as I write this) but it seems to me that writers who work with music on have learned not to hear the music. It is simply a form of white noise.

There are a lot of interesting questions about mental focus and autonomy in the presence of sound. What is it that makes some sounds random background noise while others demand or achieve dominance? I suspect that sound is the sense most closely related to our bodily and emotional state. (The neighbour's dogs are barking. Now he's shouting at them.) When my father was dying of cancer, his hearing became very acute. He would pick up words spoken down the hall as if they were addressed to him and he must respond.

Certainly there are personal differences in how much noise we can tolerate and how many levels of sound we can listen to at once. I can follow counterpoint in music, but it takes an effort, deliberate concentration.

Glenn Gould lived effortlessly in a contrapuntal world. He was famous for having two or more radios playing at once, and in his radio documentaries he used voices contrapuntally, more than one person speaking at a time. Talking about these things in an interview, he spoke of the conventions of respect and deference involved in most sound editing, how the background was usually lowered a few decibels when the narrator was speaking.

The shaping of sound shapes meaning. What we choose to hear, or what we consider worth hearing, the leading voice to which all others are accompaniment, is the voice or sound that feels most important. The ear is directed by emotion. If someone mentions your name or the name of one of your intimates in a crowded room, you are likely to pick it up. Our listening is partly willed attention, partly an involuntary awareness.

Sound is one of the ways we define the shape and borderlines of the self . Glenn Gould, interestingly, with his contrapuntal brain and refusal to declare what was background and what was foreground, avoided crowds and ended his life something of a hermit, linked to others by the telephone. He had his own ways of defining foreground and background.

If sound helps to define our sociability, it can also prevent it altogether. A sound system with earphones, a Walkman, a big radio held to the head, a bedroom awash in rock music, all these are ways of defending the self by selective deafness. The infamous youthful passion for loud noise may have something to do with the definition of the self. After all, young ears are more sensitive than old ones, so all those decibels have an emotional, not a physical reason to be.

We offer sound signals to the imagined beings in outer space. The hallucinations of psychotics are most often auditory. Acoustic space is a shapeless darkness. Sound is the most concrete and invasive of our perceptions and the most mysterious.

The End of It

The public issues that get themselves identified as moral
are mostly those related to death. Capital punishment,
abortion, euthanasia, these are the sorts of matters about
which we often wish to use an ethical or religious language, though in our secular and pluralistic society, there
is little agreement about the appropriate dialect.

For most of us, these days, morality means a common-
sense pragmatism, utilitarian in its philosophical base—
a search for those things that will tend to produce
human fulfillment—more or less thoughtful according to
the person holding the views. Abortion, by this view, is
acceptable as a means of maintaining the independence of
the woman involved. Contemporary attitudes buttress the
biological impulse of sexuality with a moral or at least a
social imperative: sexual activity is felt to be right and
necessary. One consequence of this is a number of un-
wanted pregnancies. We have accepted that the independence of the conscious being may be defended against the
life of the being-in-potential.

Euthanasia, one of the other apparently moral issues, in
fact means a number of things: the rejection of heroic
means of resuscitation, assisted suicide, and a more positive medical intervention against continued life.

I have only been close to one case on the borderlines of
this issue, the case of a man, living alone—though not
friendless—very unwell and diagnosed as having terminal
cancer, who took his own life with barbiturates and alco-
hol in just the fashion the euthanasia societies suggest. I
assume that he got the drugs without a doctor's knowing
collaboration, but it's possible that a doctor may have
known or suspected his intention. It's impossible for me
to feel that his act was wrong, or that Claude Jutra's

choice of suicide when he realized he had Alzheimer's was wrong. In the case of Sue Rodriguez, the choice of suicide seemed perfectly comprehensible.

One of the issues in all this, of course, is the priestly function being imposed on doctors. It is doctors who have the skills and equipment to perform safe abortions. The drugs necessary for a tidy suicide are available only on prescription. A doctor treating a terminally ill patient may be forced to make judgments that are beyond the scope of medical judgment. This priestly role is an accident created by our technology and our laws. Doctors who share the current utilitarian ethic will collaborate; those who don't, won't, but the amount of science they possess makes them no more able to judge a person who wishes to die than anyone else.

All of what I've just written is, it seems to me, more or less rational, but it is not pleasant. And that is the nature of the pragmatism that now, and probably of necessity, rules the world. It is, at its best, calm and sensible and very, very dry.

But what else is available? Belief, some would say, but belief is available only in a very limited way. The religious response to these social and moral questions may have passion and sometimes an intellectual consistency, but for most of us, it does not describe the world we live in.

When I was a child, my parents attended a United Church with some regularity, and the church was an accepted part of my life, but God was never, I think, much more than a word. Once when I was very young, I asked my mother about God. I don't remember how I framed the question, but I do remember the answer.

"God," she said, "is inside you."

I remember her words, remember, even, the place in our small house in Toronto where she was standing. I don't recall just what I felt, but the moment is vivid enough that I must have been shaken by what she said. I felt, I suspect, invaded, as if I had been told I was the host to some powerful and mysterious parasite. Or perhaps I felt a sense of guilt that God was there and I had never discovered him.

My mother was no theologian, but her explanation has its roots deep in the protestant tradition. From Bunyan to Kierkegaard, writers in that tradition portrayed man as a soul struggling in solitary terror with a driving and insatiable inner need. Perhaps that is only how I, with my puritan sensibility, naturally took her words. She might equally have meant that God was inside me as the source of all beauty and pleasure.

Now, years later, I would answer back that God, if he is inside you, is not God. He is conscience or inspiration, energy or wisdom. He is Freud's superego. He is the higher powers of the human mind. Such an identification of the divine with the higher human powers is the core of an optimistic humanism that has come to seem a dated and shallow set of responses. Yet life without reverence is impoverished. We are left in the barren landscape of a cautious meliorism. Or the more terrifying one of absolute valueless freedom, articulate in the intellectual as nihilism, inarticulate in most people, a fearful emptiness underlying all the chatter.

Most of us live in a day-to-day world of pragmatic judgments, valium the solution to our distress, domestic affection the highest form of love. The popularity of astrology, science-fiction, parapsychology is testimony to our hunger for mystery, for escape from the world of what works not too badly.

Without a view toward some transcendent object, it seems to me, thought can easily become imprisoned and circular; our mind ponders only the products of the human mind. God is perhaps the necessary object of the highest contemplation, and the possibility of transcendence a step toward an escape from solipsism and banality. Each of us, however unconsciously, performs life for some imagined interlocutor, and life is shaped by the audience we play for. For many, the audience is friends, neighbours, those they work with; the other voice is the voice of public opinion, and the dialogue will seldom rise above the level of banality. The stoic performs for some austere higher self, debates his life with his own right reason. The higher the nature of the other in whose sight life is lived, the more profound the living. Still, nothing in life teaches us that we will get something only because we need it.

Death is the absolute by which, whatever our philosophical position, we define life, and it is in facing this absolute that we may find ourselves wishing for some higher kind of speech—although higher and lower are conceptions that run against the commercial and egalitarian assumptions of our society, which is uneasy about any distinctions except the numerical.

In this world without transcendence, it is becoming a commonplace for funerals to be described as a celebration of the life of the deceased. No, I always want to say. We are not here to celebrate the life; we are here to mourn the death. Our activist energies wish to deny the absoluteness of death, that nothingness that can only lead to the stillness of contemplation. By celebrating the life, we can get away from that stillness and back to a cheerful and social business.

One advantage of treating doctors as a priesthood is that they are very busy people, fit priests for a very busy world. Their language is esoteric, but what they are trained to tell us about death is how to avoid it. Their proper procedures are the rational and pragmatic ones of modern science.

Where can we find a language large enough to confront

the danger and the pain, the shortness and intensity of human life? The Bible and Christian liturgy offer it. *We brought nothing into this world, and it is certain we can carry nothing out. The Lord gave, and the Lord hath taken away; blessed be the name of the Lord.*

But who can possess these words? Can unbelievers make any claim on them? How much belief is needed to have the fine old language? Too much, probably. If the whole difficult panoply is taken—as it sometimes may be—as merest metaphor, we get the language at bargain-basement prices, but religion got at a discount may no longer be religion.

Most of us, facing the fact of death, facing the public issues involved with abortion or capital punishment or euthanasia, those hard responses to the world's disorder, end where we began, with a careful and perhaps thoughtful utilitarianism; an ethic without resonance. To confront this smallness, this dryness, may be the bravest act required of a human being in our time.

Letters to Myself

September, in this part of the northern hemisphere, is more than any other time of year a hinge between two ways of life. Spring is gradual and unpredictable. From March to June, we see hints of the slowly changing season, and the change varies from year to year and place to place. September may be warmer than usual or wetter or colder, but the turn of the hinge always takes place. A door closes. Leaves begin to change colour. Flowers begin to die back. Much of what remains in the garden must be harvested before the frost.

In September, there are always jobs that should be done before winter, windows to be repaired, a porch floor to be painted, firewood to be piled in a dry place. The skies overhead as I set to work are suddenly more dramatic, layers of darker and lighter clouds blowing past, some of them scudding along close to the earth, and the first hint of night comes earlier.

September tells you two different things about time, that it is a yearly cycle, always much the same, and that your life is passing and what is gone doesn't come back. In September I harvest this year's garlic, and in a month it will be time to plant for next year. Soon I'll prune the red currants, and in a few months the branches will be covered by the round, shining red fruit. It all goes on, and I'm very aware that it will whether I am here to watch it or not. Beyond this little house and yard, the big world is noisy, buying and selling. Reputations rise and fall. I can catch echoes of it if I turn on the television set, though in blurry picture and tinny sound carried across the air as an electronic disturbance, it never seems very real.

If I never again read a newspaper or listened to a radio

or television set, would I or the world be worse off? You think those thoughts at a certain age, when you look back and forward. A man standing under an autumn sky with a paint-brush in his hand, and a few thoughts in his mind, memories, irritable speculations, I try to set it down on paper, since that's my habit.

2

Past and present. I know that I live in a world that is idol-atrous of change. I recognize that I have reached the age at which men and women begin to deliver diatribes about how things have changed for the worse, but it is just as important to put the case that some change is more apparent than real, and that the consequences of change are not what we first think, are not in our power to predict and even less in our power to control.

I like to take the schools as an example. It is accepted wisdom that education has deteriorated. I first heard this when I was a university teacher in the nineteen-sixties. I didn't believe it then and don't now. A couple of years ago, I happened to come on a *Globe and Mail* editorial on the improvements that were being planned in the Ontario curriculum. The wise young men of the *Globe* were much exercised by a low placing of Ontario students in an international math competition. Under the new dispensation students would learn to convert decimals to fractions in Grade 6 instead of Grade 7. I remember when I learned that skill. Grade 7. Or was it Grade 8? About 1950 that would have been. So when were things good, and when did they become bad?

The confusion about education, I suspect, has less to do with changes in the schools than with changes in the society around them. Television, the end of deference, the population bulge. When I left high school, it was not thought unusual that out of a large school only six or eight people from the graduating year went on to university. No doubt there were big-city schools that sent larger numbers, but university was mostly for those who wanted to become professionals—two of my high-school friends became doctors—or for those who simply liked to study. Another friend of mine went from school to work in the hotel business and was comptroller of a large hotel before I finished university—though perhaps even then the idea that a university degree meant financial security was beginning to catch on. While I wanted to learn, to be an educated person, probably I also wanted something more, some kind of success.

The baby-boom came of age; the universities expanded, and as a result a teaching job fell into my lap. The apparent decline in the qualifications of those who were arriving at university was, I've always suspected, purely demographic. If more people go, there are sure to be more who lack some of the interests or abilities traditionally required. When I taught at a university, I didn't find that students couldn't write, though everyone said that was true. What I did notice was that students with British names wrote English as if it were a foreign language, accurately, but without idiomatic fluency—a lack of the habit of reading and speaking and writing, I suppose. University was more and more a requirement for people who might have the intellectual capacity, but lacked any great interest in learning for its own sake. Education was declared a panacea, but then as the universities expanded, the job market began to contract. Then the panacea, which cured nothing, was to be replaced by a new panacea, the computer.

The present has its points. I'm writing this on a laptop computer. By keeping simple my demands on it, I have so far avoided spending time in its company when I'm not writing. It has never crashed, and I trust it never will. Now and then I reorganize a few files to create the illusion of achievement. That is the great temptation of all the new electronic addictions, of course, the waste of time in what is only a simulacrum of thought or activity. In the attempt to keep up, money is spent to fill the schools with computers and systems that will be outdated before the students are adults and serve mostly to put money in the pockets of the vendors of hardware and software. Computers have their uses, but they are no substitute for thought or imagination, and in many ways they are merely a distraction. Documents are longer, more exhaustive, perhaps more varied in their presentation on the page, but analysis will still be the province of the single human mind working alone.

New inventions proliferate, and you can be very busy just keeping up. I was late to come to digital processing, but I don't regret that. The price of a computer bought sooner would not have left me in penury, but the purchase was clearly a luxury, and for a long time a luxury that I didn't feel impelled to possess. What we do with the money we have, and how we set out to get more are defining matters about our nature. I preferred to be prudent when I might have been up-to-date.

To most of the world, e-mail and a link to the internet are a natural next step, but I am rebellious. During a year spent on the National Council of the Writer's Union of Canada, I gave a good deal of harmless amusement to the other members by being the only one there who couldn't be reached by e-mail or fax. I was dependent on telephone or, worse, the mail, letters written on paper and carried around the country by the dreamy men and women of Canada Post. It gave me a certain pleasure to be the house Luddite, though eventually I was forced to wonder if it was the merest eccentricity.

Why not move on? Look at the answering machine. I have one, which was given to me, and probably it is useful, but I find that when I come into the house, I look at it, half expecting that there may be a message. Sometimes I anticipate disaster, sometimes good news in some form, but our life is often enough lived in a state of anticipation without having a machine to multiply the hopes and fears, and what else would such a connection do? Start the day by checking your e-mail.

Then there's the idolatry of speed. Most people, it seems, are very busy, and convinced that they must be in touch immediately, but I suspect that this is, in almost every case, hyping our natural anxiety. Or a kind of vanity. We have been presented with a vision of life in which the natural competition for good things is magnified by the convention of deadlines. The busyness is manufactured. Of course I enjoy stress, activity, the rush, but I have the idea that these things are addictive and probably destructive. With the exception of an occasional medical emergency, nothing is urgent, and to believe in urgency is to be the victim of a prevailing vulgarity.

All this has something to do with my age. It has become clear by now that I am never going to be rich or famous, so I tell myself that the things left to aspire to are pleasure and wisdom. There are wonders of technology that may, in a small way, minister to these. I was foolishly slow to get a bank-card.

Everyone will have personal favourites among the new gimmicks. Some like turnips, some potatoes, but I would still maintain that the overall effect of the new wired world is anxiety and pointless rush. Of course we can't avoid the modern, or postmodern, world. There's no going back, and water will not be made to run uphill. Though I could perhaps choose to be deluded by the proliferation of goldenrod at the edge of the yard, the autumn arrival of a dim-witted ruffed grouse parading at the edge of the lawn, I know that effectively nature on this planet is dead (as the spirit of Immanuel Kant tells one of Mary McCarthy's characters in *Birds of America*). Nature is dead except in the sense that beyond this planet there is an endless emptiness that will, in the long run, win. I've never been easy about the future, at least any farther ahead than tomorrow afternoon. My light reading is crime novels, not science-fiction. As I was growing up, I saw my father repairing and refinishing old furniture in the old barn behind our house, and that helped intensify my awareness of the poetry of the past, but I know that the headlong and pellmell alteration in the circumstances of life is irremediable. Still, to accept the inevitability of change is not to becomes its slave, to forget that much is the same, hunger, desire, the fear of annihilation.

Someone once referred to my cranky refusal to keep up with the modern world as a form of elitism, and I said I hope so. However it happened, I grew up to believe that it is our business to strive to be better than we are, to avoid being at the mercy of circumstance. That could mean a splendid self-destruction, but for me, here and now, the reasonable option is detachment, prudence, perhaps austerity. Very unromantic, I know, but my few small rebellions against current fashion are meant to increase authentic pleasures, the delight of the senses, and perhaps turn my glance now and then toward whatever we mean by wisdom. It is not merely reactionary to distrust the glamour of the new, and besides, good sense tells us that its creative exploitation is the province of the young. It's their game. Trying to keep up is the equivalent of spending your middle-age racing to the gym to work out and wearing jeans that are too tight. After a few years, the dust settles and it becomes clear which inventions are useful, which not. I want to let history do some of the work for me.

3

This is back in August: a bright afternoon, burning hot in the sun, and we are sitting on a small row of bleachers, looking across a bare field where a black-and-white border collie is herding three sheep under the instructions of its handler. We came to the competition on this Sunday afternoon for no reason beyond curiosity, but as I've watched the dogs, listened to the commentator and those around us, I've begun to understand the rules and to appreciate the difference between one collie and another.

The sheep are brought out of a pen and held stationary far up the field, and the dog is sent on a long run to bring them back, through one gate, around the handler, then back through two more gates, and into a pen. Sheep are herd animals, and uneasy in a small group, and some of them challenge the dog or persistently go astray. Once or twice the handler appears to have helped agitate the sheep and made them harder for the dog to handle.

The dogs are very different from each other and watching, I find myself as excited as I would be watching any human athlete, wanting the dog to succeed, aching for it when a rebellious sheep breaks free again and again and has to be brought back. Halfway through one long drive, one of the dogs, working sensibly and with apparent intelligence is suddenly unable to move the sheep any further. The three beasts rebel and are no longer impressed by the dog's power. Then just afterward, it is the turn of a small bitch. Coming out to the starting post, she looks skulking and crushed, but once she has the sheep in her view, her power over them is extraordinary. Moving low

137

to the ground, her head forward with a snake's perfect concentration, she quietly and efficiently makes them do her will.

Experts on sheep dogs call this power over the sheep "pressure," or "the eye." What it amounts to is what we'd call in a human force of character. Talent, I suppose, though obviously the ability of the trainer to develop this talent is significant. Still, the force in the eye that makes a sheep obey, against its nature, is an astonishing thing.

Later on I found myself making a connection between those dogs, the sad failure, the startling success, and the question of how we judge our own lives and achievements, what we're born with, what we achieve. As I sat there on that August day, I was 60 years old, and it was a lifetime since I'd decided that I wanted to write books and probably be famous, and I had written the books and I sometimes noticed that I wasn't famous after all. It may be that my books were part of the scaffolding that began to be built in Canada in the nineteen-sixties and made it possible for some to climb higher. At any rate I set out to make a living by writing, and by hard work I did. I used whatever talent I had. I remember a few years back, when I realized that I was living the life that I had, however vaguely, however ignorantly, imagined, I had an oddly posthumous sense about it all. There were the books; there was the table where I sat to write them.

The man standing in the September sunlight with a hammer or a paint-brush in his hand speculates on such things and asks himself, How did I get here? There is a story my mother once told me. I was a little thing and walking down the street with my grandmother.

"Look at the brown dog, David," she said.

"That's not brown," I said. "It's cinnamon."

There I was, long before school had got its hands on me, a small poet, or prig, depending how you look at it.

Clearly my mother approved: she remembered the story and told it to me.

When I got to school, I was good at it, and I was able, just, to look after myself in the schoolyard. Probably by the end of public school, I had developed some aspiration to be an educated person, though I couldn't say how that happened. I've often wondered. For five years of high school, I travelled to school by bus, and before long, I was sitting with *War and Peace* on my lap. It seems to me I read the first hundred pages two or three times, but that it was years before I got to the rest. And how did I discover Tolstoi? Well, in my first year of high school I came upon Somerset Maugham's selection of the world's ten greatest novels. I suspect that *War and Peace* was Number One. I decided if these books were the greatest, I should read them. Dostoievsky was too much for me, and I'm not sure about Balzac—I may have read *Père Goriot*—but I actually liked Tolstoi's epic, though its length daunted me.

So there I was, a kid from a family with little money and little education on a school bus full of rowdies leading us in obscene songs (I liked the songs), and I was working my way through *War and Peace*. The school offered the opportunity, and something in my life—my parents were thoughtful people but neither had finished high school—had made me want to be clever. Some muddle of ambition and aspiration possessed me, though I chose not to seek power and riches, and I wonder now if that made my world thinner, if it was a premature austerity? But somehow all these things turned into the desire to write. Or to be a writer? Which was it, creation, reputation, both? Hard to be sure now, though it was being touched or moved by what I read that made me think I wanted to do that. I wanted to make such fine things. The first pieces I wrote were imitations—of Dos Passos, Hemingway, a poem by A.J.M. Smith called "The Lonely Land." There

139

was some pressure from my parents and teachers to become a scientist, but putting down words on the page won out, though at that age I can only have had a very unclear idea of what that would mean. I admired Hemingway and was excited by the mythology of his adventures, though by now I know that in many ways his was a miserable and corrupted life. The tools of my struggle to be male haven't been guns and rods but hammers and saws.

Of course I was ambitious. I wanted praise, reputation. Otherwise I wouldn't have persisted. To understand the interplay of smaller and better motives in the decision to spend a life writing would require a mind as bold, introspective and astute as, let's say, Mary McCarthy. We would all like to be praised for doing what we enjoy. Milton calls the desire for fame, "the last infirmity of noble mind," the noble mind being his own, I guess. I remember as a young man feeling that fame meant a kind of safety. Perhaps what success appears to offer is a relief from the terrible knowledge of our subjectivity. Like sexual adventure, it gives a sweet caress to our narcissism. If a million people buy a book, it would seem to mean that the sensibility of that book is honoured by a million people. If only a few care to read it, it is evidence of one's solitude and insignificance—but then so is the vast number of stars in the night sky.

Experience offers another kind of refuge, eventually. Invisibility creates a kind of enforced purity, a chastity of intention. I came on this sentence in a novel by Louis Auchincloss: "What is evident, at least to me, is that it is the creation of art, rather than its reception, that saves the artist's soul." Some days, I save my soul by rhyme. In writing poetry, I gave up end rhyme for many years, feeling that it carried with it an outdated vision of the world, but now, the world having turned around many times, it gives me joy to create intricately rhymed poems, precisely syllabic lines. This is in part a rejection of the rhythmic slackness of most of the current poetry I run across, and partly sheer delight in virtuosity. It is an act of mind upon the world and language, and while I like to be praised for it, I can live without. It is at least a way of knowing I'm alive. Poetry is a way of using myself while I'm here.

4

The North wind shall blow,
and we shall have snow,
and what will cock robin do then, poor thing?
He'll hide in the barn
to keep himself warm,
and hide his head under his wing, poor thing.

Couldn't say why, but I've always liked that old rhyme, and I think of it in the chilly days when another winter impends. I hear it, out of the past, in my mother's voice, or so it seems, although the voice has an English accent, and my mother, though born in England, didn't. Maybe it's my grandmother's voice I'm hearing. Something long ago.

The weather in September is sudden and fickle. Walking on the beach one evening to fill a couple of bags with seaweed to dig into the garden, we saw patches of brightness out over the sea and in the other direction the long dark veils of a rain-squall over a distant point of land. As we walked, the rain began to move toward us.

A little flock of plovers flew swiftly over the shallows, in that perfect harmony of flight that allows them to veer and turn instantly as a group, by some magic of instantaneous perception. Settled on the sand, they run on their comically quick feet. I can't quite make out from the markings, but it's just possible they may be piping plovers, an increasingly rare species now. In a generation they may be gone forever.

We live in the moment between. The rain was coming closer now, beating the surface of the water white as it came. It moved quickly, a white line crossing the dark surface of the sea, and we had to turn back and run for the car to avoid being soaked. Ten minutes later the squall had passed, and the sky was brighter again. You just never know.

Al

He was taller than anyone, or seemed so. How do you get a man that size into a few pages? If he threw one of those long powerful arms around your shoulders, you feared that he might break you. When he was over 70, he had a story about someone who tried to pick a fight with him at a party. (Finally succeeded, I think.) When I called to tell him of our friend Tom Marshall's sudden death, he wasn't silent or sad or thoughtful. He shouted out loud just one word: "No!"

Writers were always turning up at the Ameliasburgh house. You heard anecdotes about some of the people who'd parked trailers out the back. Al Purdy was affectionate and hospitable though he never presented himself as a candidate for sainthood. There was the story of John Newlove's mysterious broken ankle, how late one boozy night at Ameliasburgh there was a great flood in the kitchen and Newlove fell victim to it. Al told the story as if it was all some kind of divine mystery. Though he was a loyal friend—witness his long devotion to Milton Acorn and his poetry—he was capable of anger and a malicious wit. I recall the summer afternoon at Ameliasburgh when the name of an Important Canadian Poet came up. Call him X.

"I like X," Tom Marshall said in his kindly way.

"We all like X," Al roared. "And we all wish he was a better poet."

Al Purdy came out of the back country of Eastern Ontario, and without any of the usual trappings, education, background, local tradition, made himself into a poet. He was 40 by the time he began to have any idea what kind of a poet he wanted to be. In fact he had to invent the kind of poetry that would allow him to be what he could. Then he quit work, built himself a little A-frame on the banks of an obscure small lake in Prince Edward County and settled down to write. He and his wife went through some very bad times there, dirt poor, but they hung on. A big, rangy, loose-limbed figure with a beer and a cigar, clothes from the Thrift Shop—that was how the public saw him, at least in the early days—but he had a tough, sensitive, wide-ranging intelligence. What mattered to Al Purdy, more than almost anything, was poetry. As early as 1958, when he was still a little-known poet reviewing a new book by the more celebrated Louis Dudek in *Canadian Forum*, he said firmly, "I think Dudek can do much better, and I wish he would." Who besides Purdy would write a poem called "On Realizing He Has Written Some Bad Poems," which is, in part, about the interplay between poetic ambition and mere vanity. He was never fool enough to believe that poetry was above mixed motives, safe from the need for attention and praise; also he was never fool enough to believe that the grubbier needs of poets reduced the importance of their best work.

He went back to his old poems and revised them endlessly, even after publication. The 1986 *Collected Poems* contains at least three different version of "Postscript," from 1956, 1962 and 1965. There are even more versions of "Elegy for a Grandfather." He tried an idea one way and then another, saved up lines till he had a place for them. In the introduction to the *Collected Poems*, he gives an account of how he wrote one of his finest lyrics, "Necropsy of Love," getting out of bed late at night to add new phrases, a line from a wax commercial on TV running in his head all the while, a bizarre template for such a passionate and moving poem. I heard him recite "Necropsy of Love" at a festival in Picton in the summer of 1998. I think I have never known an audience so completely rapt.

At the end the release of breath of those 200 people was audible. Such a passionate and moving poem, but Al, being who he was, also liked to remember the wax commercial that accompanied it.

He liked complications—not easy paradoxes, but the two sides of things being lived out at once. "I can be two men if I have to," one poem says. "For being anything at all was never quite what I intended," says another one. His vision, even when he wasn't making jokes, was essentially comic because he saw more than one thing at a time. Some part of the secret of the best poems is this doubleness, the immense presence of the man, the largeness of the space he took up, alongside a capacity to see the other aspect of things "there by indirection," to look back from around the corner, to be in the present, the past and the future all at one time. The timeless kept intruding on the ordinary.

I was once unknowingly on hand while it was happening. A group of us who had driven down from Kingston were sitting around at Roblin Lake, about to eat a lunch that his wife Eurithe had prepared. Al was playing a favourite record of the German baritone, Erich Kunz. The song he was singing, *Muss i denn*, had the same tune as that old Elvis Presley hit, "Wooden Heart." I started to sing along. That's what took place. That's all. Did I look at Al and notice something? Did Steven Heighton who was sitting nearby? Should we have known that Al was in the grip of something mysterious? In the poem, published in *To Paris Never Again*, that event, the song in two languages, became one of those Purdy moments of entrancement—

a full six seconds removed
from the texture of time
not recorded by clocks
the world rotating without us....

And later:

> —during that lost time
> old kingdoms have gone to ruin
> fragments of silence
> trapped in crumbling walls
> and time enough for wind
> to pause and whisper
> a secret to the river
> something about
> a water nymph
> who was once human
> and time enough
> for every secret
> to be forgotten

There we all were waiting for lunch when that vision occurred. Or at least the intuition that led to it. Or was it, maybe, only afterward that Al remembered that moment and thought of its doubleness, thought of how two realities, two languages, were claiming the world at the same time? I never asked him.

Many years ago, Tom Marshall called my attention to a poem from *The Cariboo Horses*, "Method for Calling Up Ghosts," referred to its vision as metaphysical—I think that was his word. It's a poem about the presence of the apparently lost past. At the core of it, these lines—

> the nature of a word being
> that when it's been said it will always be said

That intuition was at the core of Al Purdy's sense of the world. He never let go of it. In a letter written three months before his death, he talked about it. "My mysterious thought is that once a thing happens it has happened forever, even if you forget or don't care." In its various expressions, that intuition was at the centre of many poems. In some of them the expression of it is historical or archaeological, one civilization overlaps another, the human facts linked through the centuries.

Mozart dying alone in Vienna
quicklime over his body
snowflakes falling gently on Franklin's men
the frozen world so beautiful
there was nothing else in life
except what they dreamed was death
the King of the Jews on his cross
composing dirty limericks for Pop
—Bukowski in his coffin
dead as hell
but reaching hard for a last beer
and just about making it
—"Lament for Bukowski"

Al Purdy read very widely, and not having spent too much time in school he didn't have a set of appropriate and deadening responses prepared. What he read became real in his imagination, blended with other things he'd discovered and was informed by his belief that what was in the mind was also in the universe. And the other way round. Every historic fact he picked up was a living human event. In the poems about history it's as if Al were remembering it all on God's behalf.

God. Religion. Purdy was an atheist, turned off Christianity at an early age by his mother's piety. He wrote somewhere that when he was a child, there was a motto hung on the wall that said, "Christ is the unseen guest in this house." The imaginative child was full of fear and guilt at what Jesus might catch him doing. Yet in spite of

Purdy's distance from any form of orthodox belief, the best critics of his work, Tom Marshall, Dennis Lee, Sam Solecki, all end up talking about religion. Again and again the poems present a kind of ecstatic experience where words go beyond the limits of time. The ancient gods remain available.

> These were the gods of our fathers:
> they are not dismissed from our own lives,
> even if we worship no longer at their shrines
> —an unused part of the brain knows them,
> when the priest's chanting dies
> and the moon silent on the silent mountain.
> —"The Gods of Nimrud Dag"

Another expression of the love of complication I've been talking about was Purdy's insistence on a wide variety of tones and kinds of language, so that the poems became a wild ride through seriousness, burlesque, the passionate, the offhand. Whether in any given poem all these things became a unified whole or whether they needed to was left to the reader to decide.

A wide-ranging poem like "The Winemaker's Beat-Etude" from 1968, is a joke and also a great assertion of some only-slightly-ridiculous life principle. The poem begins with Purdy picking the wild grapes that he used to make wine. The landscape is the familiar one of half-abandoned Eastern Ontario farmland. Suddenly the poet finds himself surrounded by cows.

> At first I'm uncertain how to advise them
> in mild protest or frank manly invective
> then realize that the cows are right
> it's me that's the trespasser
>   Of course they are curious

perhaps wish to see me perform
                I moo off key
                I bark like a man
                laugh like a dog
                and talk like God
                hoping
they'll go away so Bacchus and I can get on with it

Then he decides that cows must represent the feminine principle and soon they are lesbians, poets like Sappho, and then after a little explosion of half-nonsensical exclamations, this most male of poets himself becomes "the whole damn feminine principle" and the poem ends with one more exclamation.

Oh my sisters
I give purple milk!

As the title suggests, the poem is a kind of parody of the beat poets, but funnier, more daring and wiser. Whitman with a sense of humour. The comic extravagance of poems like this one or "At the Quinte Hotel" or "When I Sat Down To Play The Piano" is part of the great burst of poetic energy that carried Purdy through a whole series of books. One might have to go back hundreds of years to something like John Skelton's "The Tunning of Eleanor Rumming" to find anything like a poetic equivalent.

Purdy was an astute critic of poetry and in a long review of Margaret Atwood's *Journals of Susannah Moodie*— a review written during the period when he was creating the great burlesques—he reveals among other things how open he was to poetry very different from his. He talked about the question of unity of tone, and his own deliberate rejection of it. Yet not long after saying that, he wrote

"The Runners," a haunted and haunting poem of perfectly unified tone and great presence.

"The Runners" is based on an anecdote in one of the Vinland Sagas about two Gaels, set ashore in the new world to investigate the strange country. The poem presents the two, who were brother and sister, speaking in alternate stanzas. Here are the opening lines.

Brother, the wind of this place is cold,
the hills under our feet tremble,
the forests are making magic against us—
I think the land knows we are here,
I think the land knows we are strangers.

The two of them, lost in a strange place, fearfully aware of each other and of what threatens them, are the image of an alert and fearful consciousness in the face of a new and harsh landscape.

For all his enjoyment of his role as bar-room brawler, for all his occasional childlike need to be the centre of attention, Purdy had a fierce alertness. He didn't miss anything. You'd be sitting in front of the A-frame on the shore of Roblin Lake and find that he was hearing more than you intended to say. Or later on it would turn out he'd been watching when you hadn't guessed he was. It's tempting to say that telling himself the truth was his greatest strength, but he was also capable of noticing that such truthfulness was a parade of virtue that left too much unsaid. At times this catching himself up for a second thought became its own habit, but it forced the poems into new turns, making things go in surprising directions. "Remembering Hiroshima" is a poem written after he had gone to Japan to see the site of the first atomic bomb, and the end of it is representative of his struggle to catch all the available truths. We must eventually, he concludes, make a judgment.

Self-righteous and priggish of course
because whatever is most important
sad and noble or obscene and terrible
ends in the mouths of clowns
But it's all a man can offer the world
a part of himself not even original
the strength he uses to say it
the time spent writing it down
the will and the force of solemnity
are his life tho his life end tomorrow
and it will and he's wrong

For all his travel, his fascination with lost time and the gods, with big political issues—he has a poem about shaking hands with Che Guevara—he also kept close to the facts of daily life. I'm not sure if any other poet's marriage ever had such a large place in his poetry. No doubt the marriage, experienced from day to day, had all the conflicts that come with the territory. He liked to refer to Eurithe as an iron-willed woman and had she been any less, she probably wouldn't have survived, and perhaps he wouldn't either. In a number of his poems she is an essential dramatic character, the perfect foil to the clown-visionary poet. Perhaps the classic example is in "The Horsemen of Agawa," which begins with the narrative of the two of them climbing down a rock face at the edge of Lake Superior. Purdy finds himself imagining "the ghost of one inept hunter" returning in some imagined future. Then the poet observes his wife's expression—

on her face I see the Ojibway horseman painting the
    rock with red fingers
and he speaks to her as I could not

in pictures without handles of words
into feeling into being here by direct transmission

That's another kind of doubleness I suppose, His and Hers, and sometimes the poems present a comic version of it. When I heard the news of his death, I opened his *Collected Poems* at random, and there was a poem about the two sensibilities, male and female, the two symmetrical ways of apprehending the universe, though given the title, "Mantis," the implications of this one are anything but comic.

Al Purdy could write a poem about just about anything because he was interested in just about everything. Even things he didn't much like. While he was working in a mattress factory in Vancouver, he helped to organize a union, and there's a poem about trying a negotiate a raise. Another about the days when he was so poor that he took a load of windfall apples into the back country of eastern Ontario to sell them.

—in doorways of sheds and hovels
it was mostly women we encountered
(few of them young for the young
would leave this poverty-stricken place)
their faces lifetime maps of labour
wearing cotton dresses or even overalls
sometimes with faces lighted up
at the sight of those bright apples
or sullen because they had no money
and we gave some away to children
—"Selling Apples"

Al Purdy was a nationalist and a patriot, and as that passage makes clear, he knew the country at ground level. He travelled it all, a lot of it by car, but also, when he was doing journalism, by lake freighter and rescue helicopter. It's probably suitable that his last poem, "Her Gates Both East and West," commissioned for the occasion of the millennium by the *Imperial Oil Review,* was about Canada—

the country that you wandered like a stranger
but stranger no longer
yourself become undeniable to yourself
wearing the lakes and rivers towns and cities
a country that no man can comprehend
Joseph's coat turned inside out
now indistinguishable from your own innards

He once edited a book called *The New Romans*, about the effect of the American empire in Canada, and while he knew and admired American poets, the sell-out of the country in the Mulroney years made him sick.

Not surprisingly, the poems of the later years had a new kind of gravity and poise. There was no great failing of poetic energy, even in his seventies, but less of the outrageous high-spirits, and since he had become a public figure, less need for slightly defensive jokes when he thought things might be getting too high-flown, but he still kept looking around corners, catching himself in the act.

—and now far into old age
with its inevitable conclusion
I am deeply troubled
a profound literary sadness
of knowing I am using death
too much in poems
but turn about
is fair play I guess and
I expect to have it use me

153

soon for its own purposes
whatever those might be
and it won't be poems
—"Herself"

Even in the last couple of years, he was sitting up in the night with a flashlight to scribble down lines. That was his calling, what he had chosen to do with himself, and at the core of the big, contentious, outrageous, eccentric, lovable man, there was always a new poem making itself, a new grab at the huge and complex world through words.

He died in British Columbia, but his ashes, all that was left of him contained in a surprisingly small wooden box, were buried in a quiet cemetery at the edge of the millpond in Ameliasburgh. It was a simple ceremony on a bright summer afternoon, and many of those present dropped earth into the hole. He was buried under a tall green tree by poets, Margaret Atwood and Michael Ondaatje and Susan Musgrave and the rest of us who were there, and in the middle of one of the short speeches, six Canada geese came swimming down the millpond, looked things over, spread their big wings and flew away.

What's left to us is the long shelf of map-making, myth-making, love-making, hell-raising, beautiful books of poems.

Living Here

On the map, Prince Edward Island is sheltered in the arms of the mainland, the curve of coast from New Brunswick to Cape Breton. It is not quite the edge of the continent. When you stand on the north shore and look across the water, you know that somewhere out there is Newfoundland, the bigger, bleaker, more northerly island. On the south coast, where we live, near the shore of Orwell Bay with its tidal inlets meeting the small rivers that flow out of the woods and farmland, you see the hills of Nova Scotia on a clear day, and a sharp nose can sometimes smell the sulphur from the paper mill at Pictou.

Any place you arrive begins as poetry, the immediacy of new things in the new light, then gradually, familiarity comes, the everyday habits of life, local stories, the traces of the old life, wharf, church, sawmill, the track, the scatter of wooden sheds and barns from the days of mixed farming before the rolling landscape was cleared into larger fields for single crops, potatoes one year, hay or oats, onions, carrots or cabbages the next. Sheep graze, cattle, and a few horses, with maybe a small driving track standing empty in the fields under a bright summer sun. If you travel the roads of the island in July and August, you see cars from most of the provinces and states, but by September the roads are full of huge machines going from field to field to harvest the crops. Great trucks loaded with potatoes stand outside the warehouses of the wholesalers.

Born a city boy, I suddenly found myself one day out here toward the edge of the world, in the village of Eldon, PEI, fixing up a big frame house with a collapsing shed and planting a vegetable garden. When I was preparing to move to the island, an insurance agent and a fuel-oil dealer said the same thing to me; we'll set things up temporarily, but give us a call when you get home. To move to the island, in the minds of those here, is to move home, though there's an anthology of jokes about how you can live a lifetime on PEI and still be an outsider, but it's a beautiful place, and people from New York or Toronto like to come here for the summer. A second home, at least.

Eldon is still a lively spot, with its post office and general store and maybe a dozen houses standing close to the crossroads, all surrounded by farm fields and patches of woodland. It's here that Lord Selkirk brought his first shipload of Gaelic-speaking Highland Scots in 1803, in a ship named the Polly. It was near here that the famous Belfast riot took place in 1847. March 1, that was, an election day, and the riot, which took at least four lives, seems to have been impelled by those Island standbys, politics, religion and rum.

In the days before the automobile, country villages like Eldon were the vibrant centres of life on Prince Edward Island. A few years back, a couple of local historians interviewed people from the area about the way things used to be. "Eldon was a big place," one of the old men said, talking about the early years of the century. "I remember when I came to Eldon first. Right after the war. We had a bank and we had an Orange Hall and a Masonic Hall. We had a doctor, we had a tailor, had a blacksmith and a harness-maker. Right in the village. And then, shortly after that, we put up the Belfast Hall. The courthouse was at Eldon, where the Royal Bank was, and Moore's old store. And Halliday's Wharf; that was quite a business spot then."

The house we live in was built in 1896—I found a newspaper filling a hole in the back of an old mantel— and it was the doctor's house. Glenda over at Cooper's Store says it used to have the reputation of being the coldest house in the community, but every year I improve the insulation, and you can no longer see daylight from inside the basement.

Coopers' Store is where you go to find out almost anything. It's a modern version of the old-fashioned general store, and some of the arrangements can be a little informal. Standing at the counter one day, I heard Glenda on the phone to a woman in New Brunswick. She was being instructed to give the woman's brother a pair of rubber boots and some cash. The woman would be over, she said, to pay it off.

"When?" Glenda asked her. "Oh sometime," the woman said. The man got his boots and his money.

Next door to us is another old frame house, abandoned, like a lot of houses in the country here. Through the window I see dishes on the counter, a mousetrap put out years ago and still set to spring, the bait dried to nothing by now. A trap that will never snap shut, a house made safe for mice. The apple trees have run wild and produce small bitter fruit. Beyond the house is a woodlot, spruce, poplar and birch. It's a typical Island tale. When the father of the family died—maybe 75 years ago now and leaving no will—his daughters, following the path of many other Islanders, packed up and went off to Boston to find work, taking their mother with them. The last of the daughters, feeling a loyalty to her childhood, kept the house and made occasional visits, but finally she got too weak to make the trip, and her old home was left empty, waiting for an arrival that never took place.

One of the first people to stop and introduce himself when we moved in next to that abandoned house was Jim Halliday, who lives at the end of the road that turns west from the crossroads. A sign says the road will take you to Halliday's Wharf, but if you try it, you'll find the paving comes to an end at the top of a hill. A steep, red-clay track leads down the hill, through a little patch of spruce and birch, and stops at the edge of the water. The wharf, a busy place in its day with the steamer arriving twice a week from Charlottetown, is long gone, though at low tide the old foundations are visible, stretching out across the dark red sandstone. All the colours here are brilliant and strange, the variegated reds of the cliff above and the curving sandstone shore, the dark-blue shells of mussels, the brilliant green of sea lettuce, the yellow-brown of kelp.

The old government wharf, one of the things that made Eldon such a thriving town, was named for the Hallidays because it was built next to their land. Jim Halliday has memories of travelling across to Charlottetown on the twice-weekly steamer—it was called the Harland—so his mother could take him to the dentist. The Harland stopped running sometime in the nineteen-thirties, but he has photographs of it, and of the old dock.

Another of his old photographs is of a crowd dressed in their Sunday best, long dresses and big hats, and gathered in the field between his house and the water. It was taken in 1903, the hundredth anniversary of the arrival of the *Polly*, when a grand tea-party was held there to raise money for a monument to the first settlers, a monument that was built just up the road on the hill near St. John's Presbyterian Church.

Jim Halliday farms the land at the top of the cliff, still living in the house where he was born. When I looked in the 1880 atlas, I found the name Halliday on that piece of land and in fact the family history goes back well beyond that. An old story: early in the nineteenth century, the Hallidays were given this land in exchange for an agreement to bring up, along with their own children, a girl named Mary Cochrane who may have been Lord Selkirk's bastard. There's no documentary proof that the girl was Selkirk's daughter, but the provincial archives has a copy of a letter sent in 1815 from Thomas Halliday to the Earl in an attempt to get possession of land he'd been offered. He explains how he "engaged with Mr. Anderson you[r] man of business for to go to Prince Edward Island and to Carry a young girl with me of the name of Mary Couchren I was to maintain cloath and educate her the same as I did to my own Childring for which I was to have a Hundred acres of Land and her another along Side of mine I was to work and clear on both until Mary was of age and then the land to Be Divided and her to have Choise." He goes on to describe how Mary Cochrane is being raised like a child of his own, complains that in the years since his arrival, he has been unable to take possession of the land he was promised and tells of all his ensuing difficulties. He has worked as a stonemason in Nova Scotia and for a short while as a schoolmaster on the Island, living in a cold and bug-infested house. The only land he's been offered is a piece of swamp. The letter, perhaps in an attempt to put a little pressure on the Earl, makes clear that even then there was gossip in the district about the girl's paternity. In response to the letter, Selkirk wrote to say he had given instructions about the land to his man of business, but his letter makes no mention of the girl. Soon afterward, Thomas Halliday got his farm. Now, working with his son, Jim Halliday raises cattle on that same land, and in the fishing season, the two of them are out on the water to set lobster traps.

I'd heard that the grave of Lord Selkirk's supposed daughter was in a churchyard just up the road, and one autumn day I went looking for it. The church is St. John's, the oldest extant Presbyterian church on Prince Edward Island. It didn't take long to find the grave. The stone calls the woman not Mary Cochrane but Mary Douglas—Douglas was the Earl's family name—and describes her as the only daughter of Lord Selkirk. The memorial was placed here, it says, by her daughter, who is buried nearby, described on the stone as the only daughter of Mary Douglas and Thomas Halliday. Apparently Mary Cochrane married the son of the man who brought her up.

There are other stories recorded in the churchyard, lives that began on the Isle of Skye and ended here, sailors lost at sea, sometimes far away from their original home, families devastated by disease, one where four children died within a period of two years. The white frame church that stands in the middle of all these old gravestones was built between 1824 and 1826 for the Gaelic-speaking Selkirk settlers of the area by Robert Jones, a Scottish cabinet-maker who had emigrated in 1809 and ran Lord Selkirk's lumber mill on the Pinette river, just down the hill from the church. It was there that the lumber for the church was milled, and a sawmill is still in operation on the spot.

I didn't realize when I first passed by that the mill is still driven by the water of the Pinette River just as it was when the church was built, but later on I was inside and bought wood milled there, rough four-by-fours to prop up our derelict shed. John MacPherson, who sold me the wood, is an intent taciturn man. He takes his time to notice that someone is standing in the doorway and eventually to ask your business. He's been cutting up trees here for 50 years, and there's no need to start rushing now. The mill is a slightly ramshackle building shaped like a small barn, covered with shingles and painted white. In the yard piles of logs and freshly cut lumber. Beside it is the dam that holds back the water of the Pinette River and creates the large millpond above, farmland on one side, woodland on the other. Sometimes we've walked down the long road through the woods. In winter, neighbourhood kids play hockey on the pond.

As you stand at the mill, there is the constant bright sound of the waterfall below. At one side of the dam is a narrow millrace with a large pipe at the downstream end to carry the water into the metal cylinder where it turns a waterwheel. The lower floor is a wide dim room filled with big wheels, gears and drive belts. Through the gaps in the walls, you can see the glitter of sunlight on the water running past.

Upstairs, when the weather is good enough to work in the open, unheated building, John MacPherson and his two sons mill logs cut from the hills beside the pond. A front-end-loader carries a pile up to the back door of the mill and a chain is wrapped round them. When they're in place, John MacPherson slowly rotates a horizontal wheel in one corner to engage the gears in the space below. The big saw blade begins to turn, then turns faster. A pulley reels in a chain to draws the logs into the mill. There, one by one, they are rolled onto a long carriage on metal rails. A toothed bar on the bottom is engaged by a small toothed gearwheel to draw the carriage past the saw: rack-and-pinion this device is called. Then the drive is reversed, and the carriage brought back. All of this is done by the power of the falling water. The wood is spruce, fir and hemlock, cut into various sizes for building. The two by fours, unlike those in any other lumber yard these days, are a full two inches by four inches.

The scream of the saw prevents any conversation as the wood is cut, but obviously the father and sons know exactly what they're doing and need none. John MacPherson, hunched, concentrated, unsmiling, controls the two long handles, one that engages and disengages the wheel that drives the carriage, another that sets the width of the cut. One of the younger men uses a peavey to help set each log in place, and then the two of them take the scrap and boards off the far end, pile them or replace them for the next cut. Watching them, I wonder if it was very much different when Robert Jones was cutting the timbers to build the church at the top of the hill in 1824, the Gaelic-speaking settlers still just beginning to clear the land for farms.

P.E.I. has always been primarily a farming community, and for a long time one of the central institutions of any farm community was the Women's Institute. Hesta Mac-Donald is the wife of the doctor who practised here 40 years ago. They lived in what's now our house. Recently, she spent some time going through the old minutes of the Eldon branch to find out about its activities, and I heard her give the local historical society an account that offers a picture of the old way of life. Traditionally, the women met in each other's houses, "while the men sat in the kitchen and yarned." The local branch of the W.I. was founded in 1923, and a year later the Eldon Hall was built at the old crossroads, and it was in the Hall that many of the W.I. activities were held. They raised money through concerts, bazaars, strawberry socials, pie auctions, and the money went to help equip the hall and especially the local school. The Eldon Women's Institute bought a blackboard for the school, a water fountain, a flag pole. A globe. They even provided a coal shovel and a dustpan.

"Remember the orphanage at Easter," members were admonished in 1927. It was another world then, and the old ways lasted on P.E.I. longer than they did in most of the rest of Canada. Only in 1956 was the local school wired for electricity, and the W.I. was there as usual to pay the first month's bill.

There's a vacant lot across the road now, where the Eldon Hall used to stand, but in 1958, the Hall was the location of a meeting to consider building a local high school. Before anything could come of the plan, there was a fire in a school in Montague, a larger town a half-hour's drive away, and the school there was enlarged. It was at this time that the TransCanada Highway was being built, and the one-room schools were being consolidated. The Eldon Hall was torn down to make way for the new road, and the school was left empty.

It's all lyric at first, a new place, an eagle in the sky, the long twilight on the coming and going tide, and then you begin to live with the yearly cycle, the details of prose. Just beyond the side porch of our house is a huge lime tree. Linden is one of the other names for it, a black trunk and in summer a great ball of heart-shaped leaves, an old tree-house among the branches. Since moving here, I've discovered that linden is a favourite bee-tree, and if I sit on the side porch in July, I can feel the air vibrating with the hum of thousands of bees, invisible in the thick foliage as they collect pollen. Linden honey, I've read, is of a distinctive flavour. It was a popular tree among the romantic poets. There's Coleridge's poem, "This Lime-Tree Bower, My Prison," and "Der Lindenbaum," by Wilhelm Müller, which provided the text for one of Schubert's best-known songs. Much early ecclesiastical carving was done in lime-wood.

In summer, not far from our yard with its bee-haunted tree—as the crow flies, and the summer woods are full of crows and ravens, flying or settled in trees to discuss the complications of their domestic lives—the harness horses race at the Pinette Raceway, which is hidden in a small patch of woods just off the highway. We came on it the first summer we were here. The races start around six o'clock on a Wednesday evening. There's a small wooden grandstand, a frame building with a snack bar, and further off a long, low building, stalls for the horses. Everything is painted white with green trim. The oval of the track is the red ochre of the island earth, and those who climb into the grandstand sit on long board seats, some of them in need of paint and repair, and look across the red earth of the track to a stand of tall spruces that runs half the length of the backstretch. The other half is open across fields to the shining surface of the Pinette River. Sometimes above the river I've seen the quick beat of an osprey's wings, that choppy motion that allows it to stand in the air watching its prey in the water below, waiting to dive.

There's a sign for the track at the edge of the Trans-Canada Highway. It's just past Mike's Lobster Pound at the new bridge, and across from the little building, about the size of a tourist cabin, of the Loyal Orange Lodge. Pinette was the place where lives were lost in the religious riot between Catholics and Protestants in 1847, but all that—the day of two school systems, two members from each provincial riding—is past now, and the tiny Orange Lodge doesn't look as if it gets a lot of use. Cars driving from Charlottetown to the Wood Islands ferry to cross to Nova Scotia will all pass the small handmade sign for the track—the outline of a horse, the driver on his sulky behind—but most of the people who come to the track, maybe 40 or 50 of them, are from close by. The sign announcing Wednesday-night racing is put up in early summer and taken down in the fall. It takes us five or ten minutes to drive here.

A few park their cars facing the track at Pinette and watch from there. A boy takes your dollar admission on the way in, and a few minutes later, he turns up in the grandstand selling tickets on the night's raffle. Fifty-fifty, half the proceeds to the track, half to the winner. After one of the races, he will walk out on the track and get the winning driver to pick a ticket, the winner to get maybe fifteen or twenty dollars.

From the grandstand, you can see the owners and drivers, mostly men, but a couple of women as well, sorting tack and rolling sulkies into place. There's no rush to the betting windows here; there are no betting windows. No purse for the winner either. The races are just for the fun of racing, for the pleasure of seeing the long delicate legs moving in harmony, pulling the slender wheels of the carts twice around the oval, or they may serve as a warmup or training for horses that will race for money in Charlottetown or Summerside. The starting gate on the back of a pickup truck has no mechanism to fold it. Once the horses are brought past the grandstand in a legal start, the driver speeds up, and the starter and his helper grab a couple of ropes and hand over hand haul the wings of the gate back into the sides of the truck. When they want to groom the track after the first couple of races, a tractor pulls out from behind the horse-barn, with a good-size spruce tree on a chain behind it, and the tree is dragged over the bright earth to level it.

There are maybe four or five races a night—how many depends on how many horses turn up—and on the quiet of the backstretch between races I have seen a fox trot by on its dainty feet, out of the spruce woods and back in. The snack bar has hot dogs and chips, and home made muffins, sold by the kind of women you might run into at a church tea. In fact the worlds aren't far apart. A woman just along the row in the grandstand is talking about a minister she's just heard, some kind of a Baptist, she's certain, she could tell by the way he preached, and as the horses in the third race battle toward the wire, the announcer calls out, "Sing your favourite hymns."

Most of the horses here are pacers, the ones whose gait is both right legs, then both left legs. The trotters move the off legs together, front left with back right, front right with back left. It's the prettier gait to watch. Though originally the two gaits came from different blood lines, some horsemen claim that there are few trotters any more because it's easier to train pacers. Just throw hobbles on, loosely attaching the front and back legs on each side, and the horse is forced to learn to pace. Traditionally trotters run against trotters, pacers against pacers, but if the occasional trotter turns up at Pinette, they race it against whatever other horses have come in that night. It's a natural part of country life, harness racing, with a long tradition going back to famous horses like Hambletonian and the great Dan Patch, the days when the horse and buggy was how you got somewhere.

The race card isn't always planned in advance. A driver will stop his horse in front of the grandstand to tell the announcer the name of a new arrival, then remark to those of us watching from the grandstand that he has to go back to the stables to get his whip since someone's mislaid it. On the last lap of the race, you can hear the echoing sound of whips cracked against the wooden shafts, the noise urging the horses on.

At the end of the night, the horses are led to the vans or trailers that have brought them and are driven back to the farms. The sun rises and sets and the wind blows over the empty stands for another week.

A Wednesday evening, and we're sitting in the stands. The bees have left the linden now, and the seeds on their helicopter wings are beginning to drift down. I've started to dig up the garlic. It's late summer, the end of the season, a chill in the air and one of the horsemen, a familiar face from earlier Wednesdays, jokes that he's coming up into the stands to get warm.

"That one's a good little goer," he says of a two-year-old pacing down the backstretch.

No-one comments, and he says it again.

"That one's a good little goer."

Between races the driver who won the first appears in the stands, still in the helmet which is his only racing gear. He's a small, thin man with a smiling face. When they find themselves short of horses for the third race, he takes his horse out again. He wins again. Tonight, the second race had only two horses in it, and neither driver was carrying a whip. You could hear their voices across the darkening air shouting encouragement at their horses as they came down the home stretch.

There's been talk on the news recently about problems with the business of racing at the commercial tracks on the island, and some proposals about possible changes, support from the lottery commission, but nothing definite has been announced.

"They don't tell the country fellas anything," someone says.

He gets agreement to that.

"It's the country fellas bring in the bettors."

There's agreement to that too.

There are no lights on the Pinette track, so the races have to be over before dark comes out of the east over the river and the tall trees. Will there be races next week? Maybe, but the days are getting short. The air is sharp with cold. After the last race, everyone is quick to get up and move to the cars. The sun is setting over the cove at Pinette, and the beach where we dug clams in the summer is empty. At this time of year the lobster boats are brought ashore, and set up on blocks, to pass the winter, then to be painted and cleaned up when the weather warms in spring. It's part of the poetry of fall here, the boats appearing in the yards of houses down every country road.

The village that contains the doctor's house is on a hill-top, and though the island looks sheltered on the map, the winds out of the north come in fiercely. Last April, a nor'easter isolated the island for three days. Soon, they'll be taking down the sign announcing the races, but in a few months, when the ice is out, among the other signs of spring on the island, the horses will be back, their hooves banging along over the red earth.

167

DAVID HELWIG has published more than twenty books: poetry, fiction and a translation of the last stories of Anton Chekhov. For many years he was the editor of the Oberon *Best Canadian Stories* anthology. He has taught at Queen's University, been the literary manager of CBC TV drama and written extensively for radio, television, magazines and newspapers. He lives in Belfast, PEI.